The Preventorium

ULTURES OF
HILDHOOD

Susan Honeyman, Series Editor

The
Preventorium

A Memoir

Susan Annah Currie

Foreword by Cynthia A. Connolly

University Press of Mississippi / Jackson

The University Press of Mississippi is the scholarly publishing agency of the Mississippi Institutions of Higher Learning: Alcorn State University, Delta State University, Jackson State University, Mississippi State University, Mississippi University for Women, Mississippi Valley State University, University of Mississippi, and University of Southern Mississippi.

www.upress.state.ms.us

The University Press of Mississippi is a member of the Association of University Presses.

Photographs are courtesy of the author unless otherwise indicated.

First printing 2022
∞

Library of Congress Cataloging-in-Publication Data

Names: Currie, Susan Annah, 1953– author. | Connolly, Cynthia A. (Cynthia Anne), writer of foreword.
Title: The preventorium : a memoir / Susan Annah Currie, Cynthia Connolly.
Other titles: Cultures of childhood.
Description: Jackson : University Press of Mississippi, 2022. | Series: Cultures of childhood | Includes bibliographical references.
Identifiers: LCCN 2022010769 (print) | LCCN 2022010770 (ebook) | ISBN 9781496842763 (hardback) | ISBN 9781496842770 (epub) | ISBN 9781496842787 (epub) | ISBN 9781496842794 (pdf) | ISBN 9781496842800 (pdf)
Subjects: LCSH: Currie, Susan Annah, 1953– | Children—Hospital care—Psychological aspects. | Children—Hospital care—Social aspects. | Hospital schools—Mississippi. | Preventive health services for children—Mississippi. | Sick children—Care. | Sick children—Biography.
Classification: LCC RJ242 .C87 2022 (print) | LCC RJ242 (ebook) | DDC 362.19892—dc23/eng/20220329
LC record available at https://lccn.loc.gov/2022010769
LC ebook record available at https://lccn.loc.gov/2022010770

British Library Cataloging-in-Publication Data available

This book is dedicated to the
over three thousand children
who spent time as patients at the
preventorium in Magee, Mississippi.

Contents

Foreword

The Tuberculosis Preventorium for Children in American History

—Cynthia A. Connolly

Historical memory is tricky. There are few good answers for why certain health-related phenomena surrounding twentieth-century childhood, like polio and its vaccine triumph, are enshrined in our collective memory, and others such as tuberculosis and its (then much-celebrated) residential preventive and curative solution for children, the preventorium, are not. It is true that polio epidemics lasted deeper into the twentieth century than tuberculosis (TB). And it is also correct that polio attracted more attention because, relative to tuberculosis in children in the early twentieth century, it was not a disease of poverty. Polio crossed class lines more frequently than most other infectious diseases, and large numbers of middle-class children became ill.[1]

Both of these reasons may partially account for the fact that most people have never heard of a childhood tuberculosis institution called a preventorium.[2] Part of the "forgetting" of tuberculosis in the United States was due to scientists creating a vaccine, one still used in many parts of the world (although infrequently in the United States), decades before the one for polio.[3] But there may be other reasons as well. I argue in my book *Saving Sickly Children: The Tuberculosis Preventorium in American Life, 1909–1970* that remembering the preventorium in the postwar era served no one's interests.[4] Pediatricians and pediatric nurses sought to frame their specialty as one grounded in concepts of growth, development, and family-centered care, not one built around the idea of sending children away from their families to large and impersonal institutions. Scientists and public health officials had no wish to remind the public of an instance in which the science that advocated for the preventorium did not stand the test of time. Policymakers and charities likely feared that reminding the public of fundraising initiatives now considered outmoded might dampen current campaigns. And the children sent to preventoriums and their families often wished to forget painful memories related to a highly stigmatized disease.

I decided to write a foreword to Susan Currie's remarkable autobiographical journey of her stay at the Magee preventorium in Mississippi because she provides first-person insight into an important past that is largely forgotten. Another reason is that voices of children such as Currie are important to preserve. Until very recently, the only youngsters memorialized in the historical record were those wealthy enough for their recollections to be preserved in archival and oral history data. It is still rare to capture them, and, as such, this book contributes to the historical record by adding the voice of a child from another socioeconomic class.

I certainly wish I had had Currie's book when I was working on my dissertation in the 1990s and my book a decade later. I entered graduate study in health care history in the early 1990s after many years as a practicing pediatric nurse. Having entered the profession at the dawn of the AIDS epidemic in the early 1980s, I grew fascinated by infectious diseases, especially since I had been educated in nursing school to believe that I would be practicing in a "post-infectious disease" era! It is hard to believe today that there was ever such a moment, but this was the case in the 1970s, when it seemed that antibiotics and vaccines had eradicated the infectious disease threat.

While reading about the history of tuberculosis in my doctoral program, I was shocked to learn of institutions once so common that the National Tuberculosis Association (now the American Lung Association) listed them in their directories. First founded in 1909, within a decade these facilities were identified in the directories as near cities and towns all over the country. As I read more, I found scientific articles affirming the benefits of protecting children considered "at risk" for tuberculosis—a designation admittedly never clearly defined—from contracting the disease by sending them to these residential institutions. Children spent their days, including school hours, outdoors, even in winter, in an effort to shore up their resistance and promote health. They also were inculcated with idealized, middle-class American values. And the preventoriums' admissions policies and daily practices were often linked to the social mores of the places in which they were located. For example, despite the fact that the morbidity and mortality from tuberculosis in African American children was much higher than in white children between 1909 and the 1940s, when an effective antibiotic treatment, streptomycin, became available, Black children were barred from all preventoriums in the southern states and many in the North as well. Currie acknowledges this important fact in her descriptions of Magee.

The idea of sending sickly, but not actively ill, children away from their families to a preventorium captivated me when I learned of them because it sounded completely alien to the values that underpinned the care I delivered to children and families in the 1980s and 1990s. This care emphasized minimizing family disruption, educating families about treatment, and providing a great deal of support to both children and families. The preventorium seemed the antithesis of this principle. Concepts such as joint decision making with families, mutual respect, and honoring cultural differences that I assumed had always existed seemed absent. I had all kinds of questions. Where did the idea come from? How did children find their way there? Who took care of the children at the institutions? How did they and their families perceive preventorium care? When and why did the institutions disappear? And, most critically, how was it that I had never before heard about the preventorium?

As I describe in my book, tuberculosis in the early twentieth century was highly fatal, and most of those who died were young adults. Some argued that children were largely protected from the disease, but a series of scientific discoveries during the first decade of the twentieth century challenged this belief. First, autopsy studies of children who died from non-tuberculosis-related diseases revealed that many of them were infected with the bacillus. This was startling and concerning news. Within a few years, Austrian pediatrician Clemons von Pirquet showed that infected individuals reacted when a byproduct of tubercle bacilli culture called tuberculin was injected just under their skin. Most adults tested positive for infection but only some became actively ill with TB. The notion of taking the then state-of-the-art cure for TB—the sanatorium—and adapting its precepts to the most vulnerable children soon after they were infected, to shore up their resistance, was born on the heels of von Pirquet's finding. A year later, in 1909, the first preventorium was founded in New Jersey and the idea spread rapidly. Soon every community that considered itself forward thinking wanted one. Some were publicly funded, others through private charities, but they all functioned similarly. In the wake of a parent's TB diagnosis and a positive tuberculin test, children were spirited away to stay for months and years to live as much as possible out of doors and gain weight. In an era where psychological preparation of children for potentially traumatic events was rare, children were often bewildered about what was happening to them.

Currie's descriptions of the confusion and anxiety she felt throughout her stay affirms and extends the few other first-hand accounts of a preventorium stay that I have located. Currie is a beautiful and evocative writer. Reading this book, I was transported to that time and place. I felt the heat of a Mississippi summer, running around in bloomers to take full advantage of the sunlight treatment known as heliotherapy. I practically gagged at the descriptions of forced buttermilk ingestion and the requirement to stuff oneself with food. The firmly gendered expectations for good behavior took me back to the early 1960s era. Her eye for detail is so impressive that the reader truly gets a sense of her inner world and some of the tools, such as defiance, she used to cope with her stay. We learn how moving around the beds of other children and sneaking up to the director's apartment, for example, helped her become more resilient. But the reader also gets a sense of the regimentation, loneliness, and confusion of the children as to why they had been sent to a preventorium. As Currie notes, children were "alone together" and came and went from the institution without preparation. Children learned that their closest friend might be gone without any explanation when they woke up after a nap. Families visited and brought toys and food, but staff quickly took these items away. Currie paints a picture of the trauma all this caused as well as that imparted by the callousness of some nurses and other staff. She also captures the children's culture of facial expressions and other behaviors that were completely invisible to adults. Finally, and critically, Currie acknowledges that it was a white space and how invisible the suffering of people of color was.

In addition to preserving a recollection of a largely forgotten, but once ubiquitous, institution, Currie's book has an important message for contemporary health care providers. Early preventorium supporters believed that their intervention not only prevented TB but was welcomed and appreciated by those it was intended to serve. The annual reports of institutions and professional journal articles written by nurses, doctors, and scientists affirm this and often include pictures of happy, smiling children. But historical evidence suggests that many children and parents felt threatened by the idea of their families being disrupted, confused as to why it was necessary, and forced to accept it because of the unequal power differential between them and the medical professionals. However, society is best served when we recall discarded interventions with the same fervor that previous generations celebrated their successes. Doing so not only helps prevent hubris, but it forces a consideration of the intended and unintended consequences of past actions. Everyone who cares about children and their well-being should read this narrative!

Notes

1. Naomi Rogers, *Dirt and Disease: Polio Before FDR* (New Brunswick: Rutgers University Press, 1992).

2. Jeffrey Kluger, "What the History of Polio Can Teach us about COVID-19." *Time*, May 5, 2020, https://time.com/5831740/polio-coronavirus-parallels/.

3. Gina Feldberg, *Disease and Class: Tuberculosis and the Shaping of Modern North American Society* (New Brunswick: Rutgers University Press, 1995).

4. Cynthia A. Connolly, *Saving Sickly Children: The Tuberculosis Preventorium in American Life, 1909–1970* (New Brunswick: Rutgers University Press, 2008).

The Preventorium

Prologue

It was May of 1959 that you went to the preventorium, and it was
one month until I could see you. Then I could see you every other
Sunday afternoon for two hours. You were so underweight, and
you would not eat. You were sick all the time with bronchitis,
asthma, allergies, and respiratory problems in general—you were
not responding to medication, and your doctor was the one to send
you down there. I did not want to, but I had to do it. He told me
you would die if I didn't. He told me if he had to hold my hand to
make me sign the form, he would because he had done all he could.
—NELL CURRIE

1

Preventorium History

Many years ago, I was one among many of a group of discarded children who were not the model of healthy, happy little ones. Of course, we were not really discarded, but because we were sequestered far from home, friends, and anything remotely familiar, we felt discarded and tucked away, set aside, set apart, for what seemed a time without a real beginning and an unknowable end. We learned to exist in a netherworld of routine, to be wary and alert in the midst of a lulling sameness. I have never forgotten my time at the Mississippi Preventorium Hospital for Children nor the impact it has had on me.

I was a patient in that hospital that was part of a major medical movement growing out of the widespread horror of tuberculosis. Never well known by the general populace, these hospitals are now almost completely forgotten. Now, they seem alien to any modern sensibilities, and yet they were lauded for bringing children back to health.

During the early years of the twentieth century, tuberculosis was a dreaded disease that was rapidly spreading worldwide. In 1904, in the United States, the National Association for the Study and Prevention of Tuberculosis (NASPT) was established to combat the deadliest disease of the time. The name of the organization was changed in 1918 to the National Tuberculosis Association, and later, changed to the American Lung Association that we know today. Most people readily recognize the symbol of the American Lung Association: the double cross. This is the Cross of Lorraine, originally chosen to symbolize the fight against tuberculosis early in the twentieth century. The Cross of Lorraine was first used in the eleventh century by Hungary during the Crusades. It was later adopted by the Duke of Anjou in France in the fourteenth or fifteenth century, and in the early years of the twentieth century, it was adopted to symbolize the fight against tuberculosis.

The preventorium movement was considered quite progressive at the time. The movement and number of preventorium hospitals peaked during the years of the tuberculosis crisis, roughly 1900 to 1945. The name was created by S. Adolphus Knopf, MD, who, while visiting a convalescent home in Canada, noted that the routine and care was "preventive" and suggested the name "Preventatorium." By 1908, the name "Preventorium" was routinely used for the children's hospitals even as the hospital structure and daily routine were not standardized. There was not much knowledge of how tuberculosis affected children at that time. The term "pre-tuberculous" was used, although few children in preventoria ever actually had TB.

Gradually, the hospitals became institutions for the care and observation of children who had what was considered "substandard" health. During the tuberculosis era, any child deemed to be at risk for tuberculosis or suffering from other illness such as asthma, rheumatic fever, being extremely underweight, pneumonia, or the like might be prescribed a short stay at a preventorium. Early in the movement, non-English-speaking children of immigrants were often targeted to be sent to preventoria, mainly due to the belief that they were "foreign" and had an increased risk of disease.

The United States' first preventorium opened in 1909 in Farmingdale, New Jersey, and by the 1920s, there were numerous preventoria across the country, although the practices and routines varied. There was great interest nationally in preventoria throughout the peak period of the 1920s. By the 1930s, there had been much research about TB, and experts had debunked the efficacy of removing children from homes for treatment.

There was never any evidence to demonstrate positive health benefits of taking children from their homes. In fact, according to *Saving Sickly Children*, a history of preventoria in the United States by Dr. Cynthia Connolly, in the 1930s, the conclusion was that preventoria were not necessary and had negative effects on children. Additionally, there was recognition of the negative impact on the emotional health of children. In many states, preventoria were an established business, with doctors who believed firmly in their value, but due to these studies questioning their need, funding from the National Tuberculosis Association (NTA) for them was threatened. The value of preventoria was hotly debated within the medical community during the 1930s. and by 1940 the NTA issued a report that essentially deemed preventoria obsolete. In 1948, the NTA formally withdrew support for preventoria. Many institutions began to close. In California, seven of eight in the state closed by the 1940s. Other preventoria continued on. They may have justified their existence by claiming that they were created for children who did not have TB but were simply deemed "sickly." The preventorium in Magee, Mississippi, was one such hospital along with another in Charlottesville, Virginia.

The Mississippi Preventorium opened in February of 1929, founded by Dr. Henry Boswell, MD. He espoused the "Fresh Air" method of health: children, aged four to eleven, would go about as lightly clothed as possible in the belief that the health of the child would be "built up" to resist tuberculosis or other illnesses. The uniform clothing worn every day was a loose set of white cotton bloomers and nothing else in the warmer months. All children were barefoot all the time except for winter, when socks, sneakers, and a sweater were worn for outside walks.

The daily routine was rigid, with each minute of the day accounted for: meals, education, outdoor playtime, naps, even bathroom time, labeled "personal hygiene." Nurses took meticulous notes on every segment of the day. Even sleep was regulated: every child was required to sleep on their back, hands down by their sides, and head turned toward the door of the sleeping ward. No explanations for this were ever given. As children, we speculated that it helped the nurses keep watch more easily.

The director of the Mississippi Preventorium held her position for over forty years. She always met with family to admit any newly arrived patient and attended meals with the children and staff. She also taught songs and hymns to the children but was not present during much of the daily routine. She had begun her time there as a teacher and was appointed director after four years. She led the preventorium responsibly and with care. While she may not have known all that took place in the building, she believed firmly in the original idea that this care was the in the best interests of the children. Another director followed briefly after her, until the place was closed in the 1970s. The building then turned into a school for adults with severe disabilities and is still in operation.

The building was modeled on the general plan of a gracious mansion. Its front portico featured massive stone columns with wide steps leading down to a long sidewalk. The central part of the building contained two stories. It had an entrance that led to a "living room," a medical examination room, and the director's office, located in the front section of the building. In addition, two one-story extension wings on each side of the main building formed the sleeping wards, with bathrooms and circular playrooms at each end. The second story of the main building featured one high, half-circle, fan-shaped window over the tallest part of the main building and held the director's rooms and staff bedrooms. Three isolation bedrooms for very sick children were originally upstairs, but by the time I arrived, they had been moved along the hallway leading to the girls' sleeping ward, along with a small barber's room. The finished building was in the shape of the Cross of Lorraine, with the two sleeping wards creating the first longer bar of the cross and the schoolrooms and dining room forming the second, shorter cross bar. The basic architecture and shape of the building has not changed in the years of its existence. A deep red terracotta Cross of Lorraine symbol is still visible in the stone floor at the front entrance of the building.

The general architecture and use of the building, along with schedule for each day, remained basically the same for decades, but there were a few gradual changes through the years. For example, originally there was a swimming pool, but it was long gone by the time I arrived.

The 1939 informational pamphlet explaining the Mississippi Preventorium makes a persuasive attempt to explain why the preventorium is a better choice for a near-sick or sick child than being cared for at home. They insisted that consistency of routine (all children doing the same thing at the same time) would ensure a "team spirit," while a fixed routine at home would cause the child to be set apart and seen as a victim.

Additionally, the explanation is that a different routine and schedule at home would cause the child to live "out of harmony" with the routine of his family. The brochure speculates that a child might become a "small tyrant" by being cared for at home. This was one of the rationales for sending a child to the preventorium. The report lists all the benefits of a stay at a preventorium hospital:

The preventorium:
- Brings the child up to normal physically
- Turns him out a better-disciplined and better-disposed child than when he entered
- Instills habits of health and right living into him that go with him through life.

The report concludes with what a child takes with him or her upon leaving that is clearly from the viewpoint of an adult and not a child, especially the statement that "he is taking with him something that, though he can neither see nor touch is nevertheless real and vital—something that will make him in the years to come . . . more fit to govern himself and others, in short, a better man and citizen of the state."

Over the years of its operation, there were magazine and newspaper articles lauding the benefits. The Mississippi Preventorium was praised in a March 1953 *Newsweek* article, "A Pound of Cure," which gave descriptions of the children's routine and highlighted the fact that the patients came from all socioeconomic levels. The article notes, "A wealthy executive's son and the daughter of a sharecropper play, work, and grow healthy side by side." When I was a patient at the Mississippi Preventorium, some of the other children's parents were in state government, while others had parents who were sharecroppers. The *Newsweek* article also notes that there was doubt cast on the efficacy of separating children from families.

Another article appeared in the Jackson *Clarion-Ledger* with an accompanying photo on January 24, 1960. Decades later, upon finding this article, I was shocked to see my six-year-old self in the middle row of the grainy black-and-white photo. The article clearly describes why children were sent to Magee: they had asthma, suffered bronchial issues, were underweight, or had rheumatoid fever. I had three of the four illnesses listed. The Mississippi State Health Department had to approve entry to the hospital, and the costs for families are listed. The state subsidized some fees to help cover costs, but also there was also a sliding fee scale for weekly payments depending on how much families could pay: $3.50, $7.00, $10.00, $14.00. Welfare cases were supported by the county and city boards. I know nothing about any payment my mother made, and if so, how much she paid. She never offered the information. For my fifteen-month stay, she may have paid $3.50 per week ($228 total) or $7 per week ($455 total). In today's prices, $228 is worth $2,199, and $455 is worth $4,389, both dear amounts for a widow with two children to support.

Preventorium, 1959

In 1959, I was considered "extremely at risk." My father had died in 1957, when I was four years old. It's clear now that I was really suffering from his loss. But in the late 1950s, no one considered psychological reasons for children's ailments.

The Magee preventorium was firmly established in Mississippi and maintained a positive reputation because Mississippi had a much higher incidence of tuberculosis than the rest of the United States. But the institution endured long after research debunked separating children from families to restore their health. The Mississippi Preventorium closed in the mid-1970s, one of the last, if not the very last, of such hospitals in the country.

In writing this memoir, I connected with many others who had been patients of the preventorium in Magee, Mississippi. Many of us questioned the reality and validity of our histories, memories, and experiences. Many of us wondered if we had even imagined our time at the preventorium. Our time at the preventorium was a forbidden topic for many of us among family and friends. We had a universal need to have our memories and experiences validated.

A Yahoo! group first emerged in the early 2000s for former patients of the preventorium in Magee. One had to search for the group to learn about it. I discovered the Yahoo! group while doing research about the preventorium at the Mississippi Library Commission in Jackson. One of the creators of the group and a former patient had left information about the group at the reference desk. The Yahoo! group was small and private in the beginning, with shared photos and documents online. As social media changed, the Yahoo! group morphed into a closed Facebook group, which allowed former patients to connect with one another. Members who joined had been at the preventorium any time from 1940 until its closure in the mid-1970s. We shared our histories and photos and confirmed each other's memories and experiences. There are now one hundred members of the group.

2

Endless Dream

It is 2:45 a.m., and I am startled awake, feeling a sense of dread and terror, eyes flying wide open, and gasping for breath as I tightly clutch my hands together on my chest. I can feel the rapid thud, thud, thud of my heart in every part of my body. As I lay perfectly still, trying to orient myself, I see a pulsing in my eyes, a throbbing rhythm. It keeps time with my beating heart as the complete blackness of the room slowly begins to recede and reveal the sliver of light from the streetlamp coming in under the window shade. After a while, there is not complete darkness but light reflecting off the surfaces in the room so that I can see shapes of furniture. I am afraid to close my eyes again.

I am awake.

For so many years, I awake, startled in the night by unbidden memories of fear, feeling completely alone in the darkness. I experience anew the strange coldness of an institution designed for efficiency, not warmth and safety. In one repetitive dream, I am wandering alone in the complete darkness, my bare feet padding on cold linoleum, my hands on my waist in the prescribed position as I walk for what seems forever down the middle of an endless hallway. I concentrate on carefully placing one foot in front of the other, heel to toe. I can see doorways off to either side of the hall ahead, but I never reach them. I can hear laughter somewhere and the faint chatter of children far away, but I never see anyone.

I am completely alone.

I turn my head slowly to the right, trying to keep the entire hall in my peripheral vision, and all of a sudden, I see a hallway leading to a set of double doors that open out onto a portico, where the ghostly silhouettes of enormous columns are pale against the black night beyond. I am afraid to go to the door, but I am compelled to see what is beyond the columns. It takes me a long time to reach the double doors. The hallway grows longer as I plod along.

As I step out onto the portico, I look down at my bare feet. I am standing on a blood-red Cross of Lorraine embedded in the floor. It is the only color on the black, gray, and ghostly pale porch. I stop, looking down at my bare feet standing on the cross, unable to go any farther. I look out to the dark lawn searching for something, someone, anyone, but see only the faint outline of the semicircular drive at the end of the lawn, and beyond, nothing. The world ends there. There is only pitch-black darkness and nothing else. I crumple to the floor, falling upon the double cross, weeping without sound, unable to breathe.

3

Arrival

One bright sunny day in May of 1959, after Sunday School and Dr. Sims's sermon at Central Presbyterian Church, my family had a special midday dinner of fried chicken, buttermilk biscuits, and field peas that we had frozen the summer before, followed by my favorite dessert: banana pudding with vanilla wafers. Then, later on in the afternoon, when the sun and humidity began to seriously settle on the land, we drove south on Highway 49 to the preventorium. The summer humidity and heat were not in full flush yet, but a firm promise of both was in the air.

My mother brought my great-aunt Bessie on the trip, thinking she would distract me. I sat alone in the middle of the back seat, looking at the small suitcase on the floorboard behind my mother. I wondered why there was only one suitcase while there were three of us in the car.

Aunt Bessie was my maternal grandmother's elder sister, plump and quite eccentric, with her dyed red hair, bright, ruby-red lipstick, and a ready laugh that came often and easily. I loved spending time with her at her house, lounging on the huge, old-fashioned mahogany bed, her grandmother's, she said, that was so tall I had to use a little stepstool to get into it, falling into the deep mattress and big plush pillows. She often would invite me over to spend night, and she and I would spend time looking through her black lacquer jewelry box, with inlaid mother-of-pearl flowers on the top. I thought it the most exotic box ever and imagined that it came from faraway lands, but my mother told me it probably came from the TG&Y, a local five-and-dime store. Aunt Bessie would point out pieces of jewelry given to her by her husbands. She had married three times, twice to the same man. Even though Uncle Oscar had been my uncle twice, he was a dim memory. I had a sense he had been to our house for dinner, but I couldn't picture his face, only a vague image of a tall, thin man with dark hair. My grandmother and mother did not care for him. I could tell by the way their voices sounded as they said his name when Aunt Bessie was not in the room. For me, he faded into insignificance in the presence of Aunt Bessie's colorful hair, lipstick, and mismatched bohemian clothes. Aunt Bessie was not always in favor with my mother, who did not approve of her "common" ways, inappropriate laughter, and loud speech. To me, she was fun, free, easy, and different. I was glad she was along for the trip.

For a while, I rode in the back of the car, kneeling on the seat with my knees bent, leaning forward with elbows on the back space underneath the rear window, and feeling the heat of the day coming through the windshield. I wiggled one foot to the rhythm of the car as we hit the streaks of tar in the old highway that caused a thump, thump, thump sound when driving faster than thirty miles an hour. Out the back of the car, the two-lane highway was a straight, gray ribbon stretching endlessly into the horizon behind us, with white dashes down the middle and lined on either side with lush, long-needled, green pine trees. I leaned far into the back-window area to look up into the trees, feeling the hot sun through the glass. Sometimes the pine trees grew so thickly that telephone poles were pushed out of the ground, leaning askew with wires hanging. I had the feeling that if I looked away, even for a second, the highway, the forest, and the trees would overtake the highway and our car and even the three of us.

As we traveled along Highway 49, I entertained myself by making up sentences using the names of the towns on exit signs that my mother read aloud as we passed along the way: "Hazlehurst her head," or "Hattiesburg-er wouldn't fry," and even "Mendenhall is where we mend and sew." I giggled secretly to myself at each new reuse of the names.

We stopped for gas, and I climbed over onto the front seat of the car to sit between Mama and Aunt Bessie and rummaged through my mother's purse. I found my mother an endless source of fascination. Every morning I watched her put on her makeup, fix her hair, and choose her clothing. I thought she was the most beautiful, mysterious being in the world. In her purse was her wallet and an elaborate gold compact. Under these, along the bottom, I found pennies, crumbs of tobacco from her pack of Lucky Strike cigarettes, and a lipstick, which I took out and opened to see the color, sniffed to catch the sweet cosmetic odor, and then replaced the cap.

My mother and aunt talked to each other over my head.

Aunt Bessie asked, "I wonder if it will do her any good? She could get worse anyway."

My fingers landed on a stick of spearmint gum. I held the gum, turning it over to study the green paper and foil coverings. While I wasn't paying close attention, I knew my mother and aunt were talking about where we were going.

In a pause during their talking, I asked, "Mama, can I have this?"

She looked down at me holding the gum and nodded yes.

"I didn't know what else to do but do what the doctor told me. She's never been the same since Ed died," she said, looking straight ahead at the road.

I looked at my feet, feeling a little deflated at the mention of my father. I had turned six just two and a half months ago and he had been gone since I was four. I had spent most of my fifth year of life in and out of St. Dominic's Hospital with asthma, pneumonia, bronchitis, and respiratory problems. While I hated the poking and prodding of my body and the doctors and nurses waking me in the night, there were parts of the hospital that were not so bad.

Most of the nurses were kind, and I liked the quiet coolness of the room. One of the nuns, Sister Mary Roberts, brought me a set of angels with wings she had made out of the cone-shaped paper cups from the water fountain station. But I absolutely hated the shots and the oxygen equipment on my face. I often tried to talk the doctors and nurses out of giving me the shots, saying, "Wait, wait, I have just one more story to tell you."

At first, the nurse or doctor would pause, hypodermic needle in hand, listening as I made up a story on the spot about the last leaves clinging to a scrubby sweetgum tree growing against the brick wall outside my hospital room window. But after a while, they would either smile and continue or frown and give me the shot.

In between hospital stays, while at home, there was a constant battle for me to eat more. My mother as well as my aunts, grand-mothers, and Mary, our Black babysitter, all tried every method to get me to eat something, anything. My mother and Mary invented a game of making the food on the fork or spoon appear to be flying. "Look, it's a tiny airplane coming to your mouth!" I would oblige them every once in a while, but I was not interested in food. I wanted our family back as it had been. I wanted my father back.

"Well, I don't know, but it can't do any harm, I suppose." Aunt Bessie spoke soothingly to my mother. I looked up at her to see her expression, but she was looking out the car window, and all I could see was the back of her wrinkled, creased neck, with red curls lying against her skin.

After driving for what felt like forever, although it was less than fifty miles from our home, we turned off onto a road run-ning parallel to the highway, drove over bumpy railroad tracks, and turned onto a large campus. We drove along circular roads with deep, well-manicured lawns, leading to numerous red-brick buildings and parking lots set far back from the road.

Suddenly, it seemed, we were there, on a smaller curved driveway, directly in front of an enormous building sitting atop a slight hill.

Mama parked the car.

We all sat very still for a few minutes, looking at the building until Aunt Bessie announced, "Pre-ven-tor-i-um."

There was complete silence among the three of us—my mother and Aunt Bessie in the front seat, looking out the car window, and me, having crawled over to the backseat again, with half my body leaning out the window, staring at the building. Although I knew nothing about why we were here, I somehow understood this had to do with me, with my poor health. I looked from right to left taking in the wide expanse of the red brick wings on each side of the tall front section. I felt a secret thrill of anticipation, not frightened but curious. What was happening?

Mama made the first move, opening her door slowly, getting out, turning toward the building, and standing with her arm on top of the car door, looking at the imposing structure. Aunt Bessie got out even more slowly, turning sideways on the car seat, huffing a bit, putting one leg out and then the other, stiff from the long car ride. I opened the rear car door and looked behind me at the small suitcase behind my mother's seat on the driver's side. Suddenly, I knew instinctively that it was for me, but I did not feel afraid. I felt calm as I watched my mother and my aunt studying the building in front of us.

Mama motioned for me to get out of the car. She pulled the suitcase from behind the seat. I rolled the window up, got out, and stood looking at the lawn and building. In sequence, as if timed, Aunt Bessie's car door slammed, then Mama's, and lastly, mine, each slam louder than the last.

The walkway seemed to stretch endlessly ahead of us as we walked to the building, my mother holding my hand and carrying the suitcase. Aunt Bessie led the way, looking all around her at the lawns and the other buildings, chattering about what each might be. "One of those must be the tuberculosis hospital," she commented. "That must be it." She pointed to an even larger, enormous red brick building, with even more white columns and wings off to our right. I did not pay much attention to the building she pointed out.

Instead, I looked at the large, imposing, deep-red, brick building in front of us, with a wide and expansive lawn dotted with tall trees all around. The sidewalk led to a grand entrance with six enormous white columns and white steps. I could see windows in a second level of the main building, equally spaced behind the columns and a huge double set of doors in the center of the first level with windows on either side. In the steeply arched roof over the front entryway was a semicircle window. On either side of this tall main building were two long wings, each stretching far to the right and the left, with evenly spaced windows trimmed in white. The walls of the wings had triple-sectioned windows. Each wing ended with an octagonal, circular structure.

Little did I know this majestic-looking place really was an afterthought, like the children housed there, a pocket place for children to be kept until suitably healthy for return to society. I would later discover few people knew this place existed.

At last, we reached the building. Standing in front of the bottom step, I was amazed at the enormous building looming over us.

My mother continued to hold my hand as we walked up the steps. With each step, she squeezed my hand a little more. At the top, I stopped, turned, and looked back at the lawns, the trees. I looked up at the tall columns of this front porch. Wrapping my arms around the nearest column, I could not put my arms around even a quarter of it. I turned to look at the double set of doors.

We all were silent in the oppressive heat. We didn't look at each other, only at the front doors.

Mama timidly pushed the door fully open and stepped inside. The inside looked dark from where we were standing, in the glaring sunlight.

Aunt Bessie and I followed. We entered an elegant living room, cool and dark after the blazing sun. It was a beautiful reception area, full of tall sideboard tables with vases of fragrant lilies in shades of orange and yellow. I learned later this was called the "Living Room." There were deep, upholstered chairs and small sofas situated at intervals, with little tables in between. The ends of the room were curved, and on the walls, there were tall, scalloped recesses for tall vases of flowers, as well as a very large mirror centered on one wall above a table with polished, wooden, straight-backed chairs on either side. The mirror was too high for me to see myself. The room had an arched doorway leading to a hallway and other rooms and had dark, polished floors with white walls. At one end of this living room was a small wooden office desk, neat with one manila folder in the center and a sturdy wooden chair pushed underneath. A small, flower-patterned sofa was across from the desk, nestled against the wall. I noticed the crocheted arm covers placed carefully on each sofa arm. They made me think of my grandmother, Anna, my mother's mother and Aunt Bessie's sister, who crocheted so many things for us, even tiny Christmas tree ornaments that looked like snowflakes and bells.

Everyone, everything was so quiet and hushed, even when there was conversation. I could hear low murmurs of people talking but could see no one.

We were greeted by the director of the preventorium whose dark blonde hair swept up in back and curled on top. She wore pearls, a dark, smart suit, and black, low-heeled pumps. Her sweet, welcoming smile was not reflected in her eyes, which held a an inquisitive, assessing look.

The director greeted us soothingly and took my mother and aunt to the desk where they began talking.

I waited a minute to see if they would call me, and when they didn't, I looked around and hopped onto one of the chairs by the high mirror, a chair with dark, polished wooden arms and legs. At first, I began swinging my feet back and forth so I could admire my black patent-leather shoes that I wore only to Sunday school. I wriggled to the edge of the chair and stretched one leg out. Quietly, I began tapping the toe of my shoe rhythmically on the shiny floor, thinking of my father and how he, as we watched television together as a family, would suddenly bounce up and complete a funny tap dance during commercials. I continued to tap my shoes on the floor and sang softly to myself, "Pre-ven-tor-i-um, pre-ven-tor-i-um," over and over until my mother interrupted me, gently hushing me and asking me to sit still.

The director looked over at me and asked me my name and my age.

"Susan Annah Currie. I turned six years old on March 14," I proclaimed.

She asked, "Do you think you might like to stay and visit a while?"

I considered this quietly for a minute or two, studying her, the pleasant room, and the hallway just beyond the door in the center of the room and looking intently at my mother's tense and sad expression. I was unsure about the situation, even though this living room looked calm and serene and safe. I wanted desperately to please my mother who looked so tired. I smiled up at the director and said, "I will stay a week and see."

I could sense a release of tension, a feeling of relief from all the adults. Everyone smiled and was silent, waiting to see if I would say anything more. Aunt Bessie, wanting to move things along, declared, "She's a sweet little thing even if she's sickly."

I smiled back at all of them satisfied that I had said the right thing and continued to look around the quiet, dark room.

The director gave my mother some papers and then turned to me and my aunt. "I believe we've taken care of most everything, Mrs. Currie, with just a few more details to cover. Perhaps Mrs. Lambert and Susan would like to walk down the hall and look around a bit. There is a nice room just up the hall where the children gather before supper." She looked directly at me. "We call it the Circle Room. Maybe you'd like to see it."

I slid out of the chair, stepping firmly so I could hear the tapping of my shoes clearly. My mother stopped me just before I was past her and put both of her hands on my shoulders. She turned me so that I was facing her. I looked up into her hazel-green eyes and then at the full skirt of her dress in front of me. I could smell the warm starched cotton mingled with hand lotion.

"I want to see the room, Mama," I said. Her hands reluctantly left my shoulders. I was curious about this odd building and the other the rooms. A round room sounded magical.

I tap-tapped through a doorway and into a short corridor. Aunt Bessie walked ahead, but I stopped to look up and down both ways. The hallways looked so long and wide. To my left, at the very end of the hallway, there was a bright room with double doors opened. The late afternoon sun was dazzling in the long room. I could see the edges of white metal beds covered with dazzling white covers. I followed Aunt Bessie into the room with a wide double doorway just ahead of us.

The room was octagonal, not circular, with child-sized chairs arranged along the walls almost all the way around the room. Against one wall was a television on a rolling stand and against another, a small piano. I walked to the center of the room and stood very still, completely surrounded by the circle of chairs, and began spinning around. As I turned, I could see Aunt Bessie look-ing through the three high windows on the left side of the room. Turning and spinning, I saw first a half-circle of small wooden chairs, then the TV, the piano, then more chairs, windows on the right, then Aunt Bessie, then chairs, and then the door. I stopped suddenly and closed my eyes, wanting to continue the feeling of the room whirling around me, like its name, the "Circle Room." Gradually, the spinning stopped, and I opened my eyes to look around more carefully.

Through the windows, I could see other parts of the building, red brick like the rest, attached just outside the room and to the side and beyond, lawns, playgrounds, trees, and a wild-looking field in the distance with tangled bushes and vines growing up into tall pine trees. I could tell from what I saw that the Circle Room was the middle connector between the two long wings spreading out from the hall and the two short wings on the other side of this room.

"Well," Aunt Bessie proclaimed, "it looks like y'all get to watch some TV here. You'll like that, won't you, SusieQ?"

She walked in between the tiny chairs, noisily moving them apart, looking at the windows, running her finger along the sills. Inspecting every section of the room for dust or anything she could report to her friends.

"Well, isn't this a funny-looking room, SusieQ? Doesn't look much like a hospital, and I'm a nurse." She always liked to make sure everyone knew she was a nurse. After the second divorce from Uncle Oscar, she had completed training to become a licensed practical nurse, and she liked to diagnose all the ailments of friends, family, and neighbors.

"I wonder what y'all do in this room besides watch TV?" she asked.

I heard the tapping of high heels approaching. The director and my mother came into the room.

The director held out some white material to me. "Susan, you come along with me now and change your clothes."

"Do I have to take off my Sunday shoes?" I asked.

"Yes, dear, you'll get some Keds to put on later. I believe your mama brought some for you."

I left my mother and Aunt Bessie in the room, my mother going to the windows to look out. We walked past a doorway to a small room that looked like a one-person barber shop with the chair in the center and a set of metal shelves against the wall. Then we turned into a room that looked like my doctor's office. It had a metal table-bed in the center, a sink, and a tall, movable screen with white cloth panels. I followed the director into the sterile-looking room.

"All right, Susan, now you'll need to change into the clothes I've given you. I'll just be on the other side," the director said, pulling the screen around the bed and me. She chatted about the weather while I took off my dress, slip, shoes, and socks.

I held up the top item on the pile of white clothes. To my surprise, it was just one piece of clothing, a pair of white bloomers. They were the same shape as cotton bursting from the bolls, two fat rounds, very tightly gathered at the waist with two leg holes, gathered with elastic. There were no shoes, no shirt—just white bloomers.

"Be sure to take your underwear off as well," the director said.

I pulled the bloomers on carefully and plucked at them to make them fluff out around my legs.

They felt odd with nothing on underneath, and no top, but I felt oddly free and wild without normal clothes, as if I could leap and fly about in these little cloud bloomers. I thought of the book of mythology my mother had given me for Christmas and the pictures of the gods and goddesses in the clouds with pink and gold rays above their heads. I felt like Diana on her moon chariot with clouds surrounding her.

"In the colder weather," the director told me, peeking around to be sure I was getting changed, "you'll have a sleeveless shirt, a sweater, socks, and shoes to protect your feet for when we go on walks outside. In fall, spring, and summer, and inside, the children go barefoot."

She continued talking cheerfully, "I don't usually get a chance to spend a lot of time with children, except at meals and when we sing, but I always come to see our newest arrivals. I promise to come see how you are doing this first week." She smiled at me. "I'll come to supper and then to the Circle Room. You'll meet plenty of girls and boys here. Won't that be fun?"

Meanwhile, I had been twisting around trying to see how the bloomers looked in back. The air felt cool on my bare skin.

"Yes ma'am. Do y'all have dogs here? I have a dog named Tippy. Can my Mama bring her here?"

Tippy was the border collie and an adored pet, given to my brother and me by my father. She herded my brother and me about the backyard, making sure we didn't wander off. My mother had told us not to let Tippy on our beds. None of us obeyed that rule, not even my mother, who talked softly to the dog when she thought we were asleep. At night, I knew she secretly let Tippy up on the sofa and petted her. Tippy was a link to our father, a participant in our family adventures, and an important character in stories our parents made up for us. I couldn't imagine not having her at my side during the day.

"I'm afraid we don't have dogs here—there's just no room, and dogs need lots of space to run, play, and curl up and sleep inside.

"Where are all those girls and boys? It doesn't seem like much of anyone at all is here," I asked.

"The children are outside on the playground right now. You'll get to meet them in just a little while. Let's go back and see your mother for a minute."

I studied the director's face as I waited for more directions as to what would happen next in this strange place. I was secretly interested in the mystery of the quiet and the long hallways, and I felt a quiver of anticipatory anxiety that was not unpleasant. I tried to gauge her face as we turned to leave the room. But she had no expression, looking straight ahead and not at me as she went about the room, gathering up my clothes and carefully folding them.

She led me back through the door and hall to the living room.

My mother and Aunt Bessie were standing in the hallway to the foyer. The director handed the bundle of my clothing to my mother, who took it and pressed it close to her chest. My mother looked down at me in the fluffy bloomers and squeezed the clothes even tighter. She reached up with her right hand, and patted her hair into place, a gesture she used when she was nervous or unsure.

I looked down at my bare feet on the dark shiny linoleum floor. I spread my toes out as far as I could as we walked back toward the end of the room. I liked the look of my toes against the floor and the cool feeling of being barefoot. We stopped just in front of the wide double doors at the entrance.

"Well, honey, what do you think?" my mother asked, still holding my clothes close with one hand. She stroked my hair, which was up in a ponytail. She untied the ribbon and let it fall off but left the ponytail in the rubber band.

"It's awful quiet but I like the shiny floor," I said, looking at my feet, rocking back and forth, flattening and widening my toes as I came up on tiptoe. "Do I get shoes tonight? Do we get to watch *Walt Disney*?"

"Yes, to both questions," the director replied with a laugh.

Aunt Bessie motioned for my mother to leave. "Nell, honey, it's getting late. She'll be just fine here."

She took my mother's arm and gently began to lead her to the double front doors. My mother stopped, turned back to me, bent down, and embraced me tightly.

"I'll be back, sweetheart, to see you soon," she whispered in my ear. "Be a good girl. I love you."

Still kneeling, she looked into my eyes. I thought I could see a tiny reflection of my face if I looked deep enough at her hazel-green eyes. She took a little breath in and stood up.

Aunt Bessie leaned over, patted my head, and said, "Now you behave, SusieQ." She laughed her cheerful loud laugh and took my mother's arm.

As I waved goodbye to them. I felt a little tingle up my spine and a not unpleasant excited feeling in my stomach. Mysteries were about to unfold. I had no idea what was about to happen or how long I would really be here.

My mother and great-aunt left through the double front doors, momentarily letting in the white-hot sunshine and a blast of southern heat, ancient years of heat beating down on the land. I saw them, silhouetted for just an instant, two dark shapes against the light of the day in the rectangle of the door. The doors closed and they were gone.

I imagined them walking down the steps and the long side-walk, their handbags swinging gently on their arms, opening the doors of the stifling hot car, and sliding onto the seat. Then, the car would pull around the circular driveway and head back out to Highway 49.

I closed my eyes, letting the dark outline of the two of them spread across my inner eyelids. I could see their shapes with elbows jutting out sharply against the sun. I stared at this inner scape for as long as I could before it dissipated and then opened my eyes to survey my new surroundings. The room was the same but empty without my mother and her sadness.

I felt an odd relief to be alone, completely contained within myself. I sighed. I felt a deep sense of release somewhere deep in my chest and stomach. I had no need to be anything to anyone while here. I felt a respite from the extremities of emotion that roiled my home. I was now free to explore the art of internal observation.

I also immediately knew I was completely alone and without choices.

4

One Child among Many

The director accompanied me to get my pixie haircut. I remember the cool silence and the sight of my bare feet pressing down hard as I walked alongside her, only half listening to her low chatter. Being barefoot here felt mysterious and new, even though I had often gone barefoot at our house in the summer. I loved the feeling of my bare soles on the cool floor. I tried to walk so that every part of my foot touched the floor beginning with my heel, the sides leading up to the ball of the foot, and each toe. Thus began my habit while at the preventorium of walking deliberately, watching my feet connect with the floor, heel to toe, with my toes spreading, the whiteness contrasting with the darkness. I felt I could draw magical energy up through my bare feet and into my body. Sometimes I could feel a thrill all the way to the top of my head.

The small barber's room had only one real piece of furniture—the barber's chair. There was a big, square footstool at the front of the chair. Off to one side stood a metal shelving unit with glass doors. Scissors and other tools were lined up neatly on the shelves.

The barber was a taciturn man, who was just finishing putting on his white barber's smock, buttoning it at the neck. He motioned for me to climb up into the chair and sit on the upholstered box.

"Be very still," he instructed me.

He cut the rubber band on my ponytail, then ran his fingers through my hair to loosen it, and began to comb. I felt my head being tugged back with each comb through. He stood in front of me with a pair of scissors, grasped a handful of hair, said again, "Be very still," and made one sharp cut. Turning the chair so I was facing a window, he took another, thicker, handful of hair and made a few more decisive snips. My neck felt naked with no hair lying against it. He gazed at me speculatively, took a smaller pair of scissors from a pocket, and continued to snip off various parts of my hair. There was no mirror. I was not able to see my new haircut, but he smiled at me as he finished, and said, "There, you are all done now."

The director thanked him for coming in on a Sunday afternoon.

"It was the only time her mama could bring her since she has to get to work early on Monday."

"It's fine," he replied, taking off his barber's shirt to reveal a checked, short-sleeved shirt underneath. "Call me anytime you need me to come up here."

He left, his shoes clicking on the shiny floor, sounding fainter and fainter as he neared the front door.

"Well then, Susan," the director turned to me. "Let's go have supper with the other children."

We walked back through the Circle Room and into a short corridor with large rooms on either side. We turned right into the dining room which held tables for eight with one smaller table in the middle. I followed the director to a table, sitting next to her as directed, at a formally set table. I watched everyone, not eating very much and remaining quiet. No one said a word to me. I was in a daze with so many new things and people to observe. I could hear low, blurred conversations, but I mostly watched the director, who sat ramrod straight in her chair, taking slow bites of food, turning to her left to ask a child a question. She listened to the response, nodded, and then asked another child across the table how she was doing.

"Fine. I'm fine," the little girl responded and then added hastily, "Thank you, ma'am."

By now I was exhausted from the constant stimulus of observing a steady stream of new rooms, faces, and experiences. The director looked down at me and then glanced over to a nurse at the next table. She bent her head sideways toward me but did not say anything. As everyone stood up together and filed out in a single line, the nurse came to me saying, "Come with me, Susan, I will show you to the girls' ward." She took me by the hand.

I stood up to follow her as all the other children lined up at their places and walked, single file, hands at their waists, into the short hallway. The children went into the Circle Room, each sitting down, one after another in the small chairs along the wall.

The nurse and I passed through the middle of the room and by all the children. I wondered what they thought as we walked past them. The scene reminded me of the dominoes my father had set up for my brother and me in a straight line, falling one by one.

The hallway to the girls' ward was long and empty. We passed the room where I had changed and another that looked like a hospital room. I turned my head away as I did not want to see another hospital room. I had spent way too much time in St. Dominic's Hospital when I was five.

Just before the entrance to the girls' ward, there was an open cupboard door in the wall to my left. The shelves held stacks and stacks of white material. I looked intensely at the shelves seeing white sheets, white pillowcases, and white bloomers and shirts.

As we arrived at the girls' ward, I stood in the middle of the wide double doorway and gazed at a deep, rectangular room that reminded me of a hospital ward. It had a double row of low lockers down the middle. Rows of beds were along both walls, stretched throughout the room, with huge, tall, triple-paned windows above them. Some of the windows looked out onto the front lawns while the back-wall windows looked out to the space between this wing and the shorter back wing. I could see the windows of the Circle Room to the right. The windows were unlike any I had ever seen, twelve to each side of the long room, designed to be opened to the ceiling and with internal shutters with moveable slats.

Just inside the doorway was a nurse's station, which was a small desk with a lamp on it. Across the room from the nurse's station, a door led to the showers and bathrooms. Grey metal lockers were set back-to-back in groups of four down the middle of the room to provide division but also to allow easy access to either side. Each child had a locker with three sets of pajamas, a pair of socks and sneakers, a sweater, a comb and brush, and a toothbrush. This was what had been in the small suitcase my mother carried in. I had not been present when she or someone else had put my few belongings in my locker. My name was on the locker, and the pajamas in it had my name stamped inside. Earlier that week, I had seen the small, black wooden stamp on my mother's dresser.

That first night, even though I was exhausted by curiosity and confusion about this place, I lay in my white bed and could not fall asleep. The nurse had not been unkind, just matter-of-fact. She had taken me into the bathroom to a lavatory, instructing me to brush my teeth, put on my pajamas, and get into bed. She told me that I would join the children in the Circle Room the next day. She also instructed me to lie on my back with my head turned toward the nurse's station to my left. I lay in the bed with my head turned obediently, watching and listening as the girls pattered in, went to their lockers, took off their bloomers, and put on their pajamas. They lined up to brush their teeth and then climbed into their assigned beds. At first, they murmured and chattered in low voices, but they all quieted down quickly when the nurse walked around the ward. I lay thinking about each little girl in the ward, wondering what they were thinking and feeling and why I had to lie in bed a certain way. I tried to imagine what would happen the next day.

I closed my eyes but not quite all the way, and by squinting my eyelids, I could see areas of the long room. I watched the nurse at her desk, writing. After the ward became quiet and the twilight sky darkened, she got up and went out the door. I immediately took the opportunity to try and lull myself to sleep as I did every night by very gently rubbing and tapping the soft pad of my little finger against my lower lip.

This was a habit I had developed as a baby and continued as I became a toddler and older. It reminded me of my father who often, coming home at the end of the day, swept me up in his arms while taking his own little finger and tapping it against his lower lip in sync with mine.

"How we doing, my little SusieQ? Why are we tapping our lip? Is this your thinking process?" He would laugh and put me down, and the family evening would begin.

It was the only way I could fall asleep. But I knew to stop when the nurse came back through the doors.

I must have finally fallen asleep that first night as I lay in this stark new world.

I awoke the next morning to a ringing bell, opened my eyes, and looked around me. The room seemed enormous. At the very end, I could see another set of wide double doors that led to a smaller room in the shape of a semicircle. Closed cupboards and closets held mysterious contents, and shelves displayed toys that we were allowed to play with only at assigned times.

I stared at the beds again. They were brilliant with blindingly bright white sheets. Some beds had coverlets with a deep red double cross emblem down the middle. The beds with these coverlets were unoccupied. I did not know it at the time, but this was the Cross of Lorraine, symbol of the tuberculosis movement. The coverlets echoed the enormous deep red double cross embedded into the middle of the pavement in front of the entrance to the preventorium. I loved the blood-red symbol, which looked mystical and dramatic to me. I did not know that, to the majority of the population at large, it was a dreaded sign of disease.

I stared at everything, trying to imprint all the details in my mind so I could remember them, not realizing that I would dream of them almost every night once I left. But then, in this moment, I could not imagine getting used to this place, so brilliantly bright with the windows, the white sheets, and our white, cloud-like bloomers. This was the first day of the daily and nightly routines, repeated on an endless loop for the entire time I was at the pre-ventorium. As my time there lengthened, I remembered thinking I had been caught in a time warp or was cursed to repeat the same day over and over.

That bright May morning, I listened to the noise of the con-versations, lockers opening and closing, girls giggling, one or two crying, the sound of bare feet slapping against the floor as they jumped out of their beds.

I did not immediately jump out of bed. I reached for my long hair, forgetting that my ponytail had been cut. I ran my hand slowly over the nape of my neck feeling the fuzz. I wondered if the barber got bored giving every girl short bangs and the straight blunt cut that stopped just below the ears and giving every boy a short, bristly crew cut. Was it interesting when a girl had curly, curly hair, like the little girl and her sister that I noticed in the dining room last night? I didn't know their names yet, but I gave them imaginary names. This was a game I often played, looking at people and deciding what name they "looked like." I named the older sister with the curly black hair "Diana" and her little sister, who had wavy brown hair, "Nan." The imaginary names stuck in my mind. "Nan's" hair waved out on each side of her head like angel wings. The rest of us girls had shiny caps of straight, silky hair that swung free.

No adult told me what to do on that first morning. I followed the other girls, got out of my bed, and stood next to it, uncertain of what to do next. I watched and followed as one went to her locker, took out a toothbrush and went to receive a facecloth, then to line up in front of a large communal bathroom. I too went to my locker and reached for my toothbrush on the top shelf. It was a small, new, pink one. I walked toward the line of girls, some sleepy and rubbing their eyes and faces, some chattering away. I peered around them to see that the bathroom had five sinks, two very elevated large bathtubs with steps, and a separate shower room off to the side. There were five enclosed toilet stalls in another area. As I waited in line to wash my face and brush my teeth, I looked down at my bare feet and listened to the general hum of noise. The little girl behind me poked me, and I saw that the line had moved forward.

She asked me, "Did your parents leave you here yesterday? I saw you walking through the Circle Room last night. What is your name?"

Without even waiting for my response, she pointed at the two nurses, telling me which one was nice and which was not.

Four little girls stood at white sinks set low so that they were easier to reach. They washed their faces and brushed their teeth, splashing water, and then moved to the toilet stalls.

When it was my turn at the sink, I copied the little girl next to me. I folded my washcloth into a square like she did, then held only the tip end of the corner of the square under the water so that the cloth got wet only at the top part to the middle.

Smiling at me, the little girl whispered, "This is so water doesn't drip down your arms."

Two nurses stood at the doorway to observe everyone. Each held a clipboard and questioned each little girl coming out of the toilet. They wrote furiously on the clipboard to record the answers. When it was my turn, I was shocked to hear the question asked of me.

"Number 1 or number 2?" they asked.

I stopped still, shocked at the question. I thought this was none of their business, but an inner instinct warned me to reply. I mumbled my answer, looking down at the floor. One of the nurses, young and pretty with smooth blonde hair pulled back underneath her white cap, smiled at me, asked my name, and wrote my answer down.

"Yep . . . they write down every time we go to the bathroom. You have to try hard sometimes. One of my friends had to sit on the toilet all afternoon once before they finally let her go to supper," the little girl behind me whispered as I joined the line again. Horrified at the thought, I watched the other children as the questioning continued.

Finally, our teeth were brushed, faces were washed, and our "personal hygiene" completed. Then, still in pajamas, we all walked out into the hallway and lined up in front of the open cupboard in the wall.

One by one, we stepped in front of the nurse, putting our open palms together, like an offering. Then the nurse gave each of us a pair of white bloomers. This was rhythmically repeated: the nurse reaching in, taking out a pair of bloomers, placing them on the open palms of the little girl in front of her, who then went back into the ward to put them on, while the next one behind her stepped forward to receive her bloomers.

I followed along, imitating the others. In my fresh, clean bloomers, I stood, observing the busy, bustling room, and listening to the sound of locker doors closing.

For many children at the preventorium, though, the bloomers were a badge of shame, embarrassing and worrisome in their looseness, for we wore no underwear. I thought they were wonderful; I enjoyed the freedom from heavy clothing. I wouldn't have minded running naked, but the preventorium staff had a limit—bloomers were always required except for sleeping, when we wore pajamas. In cooler weather, we had white, cotton, sleeveless, vee-necked shirts, and in fall and winter, we had a three-quarter-sleeved sweater to wear outside, along with sneakers and socks. But most of the time, we just wore the bloomers. Thankfully, I never saw anyone try to pull down another child's bloomers as a joke. We were all in the same situation, and besides, shame was more likely to come from an adult than another child.

Someone must have ironed all those clothes as we were given fresh sets each day. The sleeveless vee-necked shirts worn in cooler weather never had one wrinkle, even after vigorous playtimes. The color white was everywhere.

Only our schoolteacher wore any color she desired. The director, too, could freely choose any fashion or color she fancied.

In the summer, we looked like little stick figures puncturing dozens of white cloud bloomers. Photos of us are startling and unsettling to viewers. How odd it must have been to see a room full of children in little fluffy white bloomers, all arms and legs and bare feet.

The daily routine is burned into my brain. Morning after morning, we removed our pajamas, folded and placed them in our lockers, then unashamedly pulled on our bloomers and gathered in the hallway.

We were all little clones with the same haircut and those white bloomers. That first day, I loved the newness of the bloomers and the ease in getting dressed. I loved fashion and clothes, but this was so new. It was liberating to feel so bare, so close to complete nakedness. Over time, as visitors came to see us, their clothes and shoes looked strange, uncomfortable, and restrictive to me.

◆ ◆ ◆

After dressing, it was time to go to breakfast in the dining room.

"Okay girls, time to line up, single file please, with your hands at your waist, and follow me," the older, stern nurse said sharply with a frown of her dark eyebrows.

We followed her instructions. There we were, nineteen or so little girls, all with the same bad haircut of short bangs, in differing heights, all in fluffy white bloomers and nothing else, in a somewhat straight line with our arms akimbo. Three or four older girls, ten or eleven years old, were allowed to wear the sleeveless vee necked shirts all the time.

"Put your hands on your waist," said the still-nameless little girl who had accompanied me for the morning routine. "We always have to do that." She smiled and demonstrated as she put her hands on her waist.

"Okay. Like this?" I placed my hands on my waist making sure my elbows stuck out on either side. She nodded yes.

The nurse looked us over, turned abruptly, and headed down the hall. We followed her until we met up with a similar single file of little boys, with closely shaved buzz cuts. We all looked like tiny wobbly robots, stiffly walking with our thin arms and legs, a puff of white in the middle of each little body. It would have been difficult to differentiate girls from boys if not for our distinctive haircuts.

The two lines of boys and girls slowly merged, heading toward the Circle Room. The nurse at the head of each line tapped the shoulder of the child next to her, to indicate that he or she was to enter. We each waited our turn, interfiling into one combined line of boys and girls. This was our method of going from one place to the next—and always in single file with hands on hips, to keep us from getting into any trouble.

We rebelled by turning our hands with our fingers pointing backwards instead of forward. We would glance behind us at friends and smile significantly to indicate that we were NOT following instructions! But woe betide the child who was in any way different. So, we were careful and quick not to be caught with our arms in an incorrect position.

One of the strongest memories I have is the countless waking hours of walking in single-file lines.

How strange this was at first—lining up, silent, with my hands on my hips, trying not to turn around to see what was happening behind me. I had a sensation of being in an alternate universe. We were a group of many, but each of us was so alone. It's not that the staff was actively unkind in most of the routine procedures, but they were trained to keep us in order, to follow the rules. All of us behaved and acted the same way.

But none of us were the same. We were all strangers to each other, taken from home for reasons we did not understand and with few opportunities to truly make friends. Simply our being roughly the same age and in the same situation does not automatically make for friendship. Inside this blazing white building, locked away from the world, I stood in line separated as something other than normal.

That first morning, we marched through the hallway, through the Circle Room, and turned right into a formal dining room.

The dining room was large, brightly lit, and airy. There were eight long rectangular tables, each set for eight to ten persons with a tablecloth, white cloth napkins clinched in little silver rings placed at the top of the plates, formally placed silverware and dishes, and a small flower arrangement in the middle. The tables were arranged in a large U shape around the room, with a smaller table in the middle, upon which sat an enormous seasonal flower display. One of my favorite activities was studying the floral arrangements in the dining room.

In the spring, there were wisteria, daffodils, and tall ferns; in the fall, artistically arranged branches with leaves, branches with sweetgum balls, and perhaps some late-blooming Queen Anne's lace. For the winter holidays, the arrangements included holly and buttonbush, along with poinsettias. In spring and summer, the flower arrangements were lush and wildly extravagant, with lilies of all colors, magnolias, forsythia, and jasmine, which perfumed the dining room.

The fragrance that first morning was of flowers that had been left just a day or two too long—a pungent, not-quite-rotten odor underneath the opulence of lilies, which had the slightest tinge of brown. The scent reminded me of the funeral home during calling hours for my father in a room overfilled with stands of carnations and lilies. I wrinkled my nose at the memory.

By the time we had our midday meal that day, the flower arrangement had been changed.

Behind the flower display table was a set of double doors with windows, leading to the kitchen, behind which I could see people with white caps bustling about. Sometimes one of the workers would come to the square window to gaze out at us in the dining room.

Dining room, courtesy of Elsa Clift Everling

As we filed into the dining room, the first six or seven children went to the table the furthest away from the door. Each stopped at a place setting and stood at the table, hands on the backs of their chairs, waiting until everyone was in the room and seated. A nurse, teacher or aide sat at each table. We waited until the director was at her chosen place. A small silver bell was placed above her plate. She gently picked it up and gave it a little shake so that it trilled throughout the room, and we all sat down together. Then the director or a nurse said grace for the meal. I bowed my head but glanced to either side to see who else was following along. Many children had their heads bowed very low but did not have their eyes closed. They stared at their hands in their laps or at the plate in front of them. Some children seemed as if they might fall back asleep. After the blessing, platters of food were brought in.

The meal routine was always the same. We stood until everyone had arrived and sat in unison on the director's command. We remained motionless until she rang her bell. Then, all together, we grasped our napkin rings with our left hands, extracted the cloth napkins with the right, and placed them in our laps. When she was satisfied that every napkin was in an identical position, she rang the bell again. Then we could talk, but we still waited for the adult at our table to pick up her fork before we took our first bite. And the bell always rang again randomly at a time of the director's choosing. That second bell meant instant cessation of chatter, even mid-word. I found this frustrating at first as I wanted to either finish what I was saying or didn't want to talk at all. But my mother had told me that part of the preventorium's mission was to teach "good manners and social graces," as she called it. Being able to make conversation was encouraged as part of that mission. Looking back, it would have been better if they had taught us to remember how to tell time and understand more math. But polite conversation at meals was considered a must. We never learned why conversations were stopped at times during meals.

At breakfast, we invariably had eggs in some form, usually scrambled, bacon, a platter of toast or biscuits, fruit, a glass of deeply yellow milk, and another of water. I sat quietly that first morning, listening to the nurse ask questions, which the children at my table dutifully answered. I moved the food around on my plate and tentatively tasted the milk, which I almost spat out. Instinct told me to eat and drink, but I did not like any of it at all. As I was new, the nurse at my table watched me but did not insist that I eat everything. Over time, I battled the adults over the food served, but in those first days, I watched and obeyed. At any given moment, I had already learned, the bell would ring again, which meant all conversation would cease and the meal would continue in silence, with only the clinking sound of silverware against china.

When the bell rang out again, this time a little longer, everyone quickly rolled up his or her napkin and replaced it in the little ring above their plate. The meal was ending. We sat at the same places for our noontime dinner and evening supper, but the next day, we might be moved to a different table. One day, we might be with a nurse, another day at the director's table.

That first morning, as we went about our morning ablutions, I heard the nurses talking to each other about the strict routine.

"You know the doctor who founded this place believes in the benefits of routine and consistency help to establish good habits," one nurse said to the other.

In retrospect, I know that consistency can lead to establishing bad habits too. Good habits were certainly the plan at the preventorium, but the rigidly strict routine stamped out a good amount of normal child development and individuality. No one was encouraged to be different or unusual in any way. In fact, we were all rigorously forced to conform to rigid behaviors with no crying or normal playfulness allowed. Over time, some children developed nervous tics and habits like the little boy who, if you dared to look at him directly, threw his arm across his eyes, as he strove to avoid direct eye contact. Whenever anyone approached him, tried to take a photo, or simply talk to him, he turned around or ran away, covering his eyes.

"Why?" I wondered. "What happened to him? Did it happen at the preventorium?" He always ran from cameras on visiting Sundays, when parents and families often took photos of their children with toys. But I never saw him with a family. Some children did not have visitors. These were the saddest children at the preventorium, withdrawn and alone. Over time, I could see a difference in how they were treated by the staff. Some received harsh punishment, and others were simply ignored. It was easy to see those children whose families visited regularly were treated better.

It was a strange, cold, and disorienting experience being forced into sameness. There were no choices allowed us, no individual spark or quirky differences tolerated. Although I longed to be unique, to be myself, I instinctively knew I had to conform. I also wanted to please my mother, the nurse, the director, or any adult near me.

The strict daily schedule was included in materials given to parents and was adhered to every single day. Sometimes I had the feeling of being caught in a time warp of sameness: hearing my feet plop on the floor each morning, the ritual hand and face washing, the recording of our "personal hygiene" sessions, then breakfast, school for half a day except in summer, the welcome relief of running outside to play, which was the only time of released nonconformity, then noontime dinner, an afternoon nap, the afternoon milk, another playtime outside, supper at 6:00 p.m., a story hour or TV time, and finally, evening bath (for young children, showers for six and older), and bed by 8:00 p.m. Every movement was meticulously watched and recorded. "Personal hygiene" breaks were regularly interspersed throughout the day. On Sundays, we often had Sunday School morning devotional time with the singing of hymns, and then after noontime dinner, parents and adult family members could visit for two hours. We called them "visiting Sundays."

On visiting Sundays, some children cried every time their parents arrived and left. I watched them impassively. I understood it did no good to weep when the parents all had to eventually leave. My mother always looked sad as she hugged me, but then she always smiled. It transformed her face completely. She wanted me to picture her smiling, she told me. And I did. And eventually, I came to realize that my father was never coming home. I learned that loss could happen instantly.

◆ ◆ ◆

As I had been admitted to the preventorium in late May, the regular school year ended soon after my arrival. I was happy to enjoy summer recess so soon. It meant more playtime, a longer time outside in the mornings instead of a short break after classes, and in addition, we also had the usual play time in the afternoon.

Playing out of doors was the one time—the ONLY time—when all of us veered close to riotous, uncontrollable behavior. It was the one time our natural personalities were allowed to emerge. Running in all directions at once out of the back door between the schoolrooms and dining room and then down the steep concrete steps, some children dashed to the swing set and seesaws. Others headed toward a small shed, called the "Brown House," where outdoor toys and craft supplies were stored, including balls of all sizes, stick horses with yarn manes and felt ears, jump ropes, and art supplies.

Some days many of us just ran around the playgrounds, letting off pent-up energy. I often chose to go alone beyond the boundaries of the playground, into the tall grass and wildflower fields out behind the closely mown green lawns. I ventured as far as I could from the nurses and the noise of children shouting, running, and jumping. I wanted time to myself.

I ran my hands over the tops of wild, fragrant pink and purple phlox, ox-eye daisies, orange milkweed, and the black-eyed Susan flowers that reminded me of my father. He had told me they were planted everywhere just for me. There was honeysuckle too, and I often plucked the delicate stems off the flowers to taste the tiny drop of nectar inside. Beyond the fields, I could see thick pine trees growing closely together, suffocating and choking everything. This was known as the "Piney Woods" region of the state. The soil was too sandy for farming, but logging the pine trees had become a part of the national timber industry.

I lay down in the tall grass and flowers so that I could just barely see the heads of others on the playground. I loved to watch children on swings appear and disappear in a lulling rhythm. They would fly upwards toward the sky, their bare feet high in the air, and then back down to the earth, disappearing for a moment, and then suddenly they were rising into the air again. Often, too, I could glimpse others on the seesaws. I counted each time one of the little cropped or buzzed heads appeared as they went up and down. I thought about how similar the movements of the swings and the seesaw were. The steady, rhythmic movement hypnotized me, and I nearly fell asleep sometimes.

I stared into the distance, allowing my eyes to glaze over, making everything hazy. As my eyesight blurred, my imagination took over and I pictured otherworldly creatures, just outside my direct line of vision, a magic leaping shadow or a tiny, sparkling being, quickly moving through blades of grass. Perhaps it was one of the Greek naiads that I had read about in my favorite mythology book that my mother had given me for my birthday. She had explained the word "naiad," and we pronounced it aloud together. I loved saying it over and over out loud as I wandered about. Or maybe it was a wood nymph dashing between flowers and trees, invisible unless you were looking away: the wings of the nymph flashed by your eyes, and you only saw them as an afterthought. I was always looking for fairy wings. Dragonflies were rare sightings of fairies not wishing to be seen. I followed them as far as the rough ground outside the well-maintained play area would allow, finally stopping when burrs from wildflowers began scratching my bare legs in the sticky heat.

Heat in Mississippi is heavy and deep. It is absorbed by and into everything: bricks, concrete, glass, and especially metal. All absorb and retain the heat. It settles more than temperature over the environment. There are days when it is so thick in the humid air that everything slows imperceptibly. The trees, stewing in the humidity seem to have resigned and sit, aging in the endless summer. The heat slowed us down too. On the playground in July and August, we sat languidly in swings, turning and drifting, allowing our bare feet to drag in the hard-packed dirt and grass. Other children would stretch out in grassy areas, gazing up at the clouds and the searing blue of the afternoon sky. The nurses sat with paper fans on the outer benches, ignoring the children, except when one of us breached the perimeter. The intense weight of the heat fell over us, and we were all silenced by the oppressive sultriness. That ancient and persistent heat held everything still, with time stopped forever. We were incandescence itself, burning brightly in the tiny, isolated town of Magee.

In the heat, I daydreamed about secret, magical worlds that would reveal themselves to me if I was quiet and attentive enough. I watched shafts of sunlight between the trees, waiting for the sparkle of a world opening. I was certain I would eventually find a way into that bright world, far away from the preventorium.

Drowsy from the sun and heat, hyperaware of the scent of wildflowers and soil, the hum of a bee, the faraway laughter and chattering on the playground, I treasured these solitary minutes.

Time is relentless even when it seems to stand still. When there is the same, specific routine day after day, hour after hour, night after night, unique moments make certain times stand out from the blur of the daily drill. I felt eternity in the small, still moments.

We were trapped here, and no one was coming for us. There was a sense of release in knowing that we had no options, a relief in the submission to the inevitable. Isn't that what prisoners or trapped animals feel eventually—a giving up?

I had no sense of the outside world nor any knowledge of what might be happening beyond the preventorium. I was nonessential. The world did not need me or any of the other children.

We were caught in a universe of precise routine yet had no sense of time passing in any meaningful way. We had no knowledge of our homes either. We had only an ultra-bright hospital existence that pretended to be a home for us.

While I was at the preventorium, I developed a habit of always waiting. Others did also, perhaps.

I waited for playtime so I could be silent and alone or run and talk as much as I wanted. I waited for the precious few hours watching TV so I could escape into another world. I especially loved Sundays when we watched *Walt Disney*, as there were frequently fairy tale or cartoon fantasies.

I waited for class time so I could read as many books as possible. On visiting Sundays, like everyone else, I waited for my mother, who nearly always brought gifts that I didn't get to keep. Sometimes she would bring a neighbor or a friend with her.

I waited for letters and postcards. I waited to write postcards. I waited for naptime to think, to be still, to daydream, and escape to my inner fantasy world. I waited to get up for playtime outside.

As time passed, I didn't wait to go home. That was unknowable and never mentioned by any nurse or staff to anyone.

I became at once extroverted and introverted—both necessary for survival, a miniature, two-faced Janus, entering the portals of extreme isolation. In this group setting, I was alone. So was every other child. And those children whose families could not visit were especially isolated.

I could bring an inner secret fantasy world alive at a moment's notice with whatever was at hand. I found a broken piece of colored glass, the bottom of an old, pale-green, Coca-Cola bottle, on the playground. I held it up to the light, close to my eyes, blotting out everything except the thick, pale-green bottle bottom. When the wavering light shone through the filmy, viridescent glass, I could see another world. I hid this broken glass from the nurses who would have surely take it from me. Through its small, rough magnifier, I saw translucent green trees, pale and yellowish if the sun shone brightly, and the distorted wavy, ruffled shutters on the buildings. I saw blurred images transformed into animals that moved slowly or quickly, depending on how fast I moved the glass back and forth. I loved taking the thick fragment of glass and peering through it. It was the entrance to my mystery world in the forest, a portal where trees lined up, waving their branches as if underwater, a beckoning forest hallway inviting me to enter a deep, magical world.

On Sunday, when my mother arrived for the short afternoon visit, I would pull her diamond ring off and hold it close to my eyes. Upon first staring at the tiny, tiny reflections in a diamond, one sees nothing. But upon gazing longer, things take shape. There is a miniature reflection of a tree blowing in the wind, my own eye looking back at me, the striations of my iris huge and close. Or I would take out the powder compact from my mother's purse and hold the mirror upwards, while walking looking and into the mirror. This created yet another world for me, one where I strolled among the treetops and through the sky. When I did this inside a building, I stepped "over" doorways and light fixtures. Sometimes when I held the mirror to reflect only the sky, I felt momentarily disoriented as if I would suddenly fall "up" into the sky.

At other times, I was very talkative and social, organizing play for others based on the few television shows we watched: *Walt Disney* and *Rawhide* or *Roy Rogers*. When choosing toys for afternoon playtime, I always took the broomstick ponies with toy horse heads, yarn manes, and huge, round eyes. Then I rounded up a group of children who also had chosen broomstick ponies so we could play "American Revolution," riding our horses through the countryside to gather our forces for the oncoming battle.

Sometimes, we were homesteaders, heading for a new land in which to settle down and create a new home. I assigned one or two others to pretend that they were sitting on high wagon seats and two more children to prance in front of them as horses leading the wagon. If I was pretending to be sitting upon the wagon seat, I would dramatically crack the whip, and imitate a snapping noise. "Get along now. . . . We have to make camp before nightfall," I would call out. These games seemed to go on for hours, although in reality we only had a short playtime each day.

Given the sudden and sometimes confusing freedom from our strict routine, many children seemed happy for someone to organize play and activities. I herded us through the fields and play area, devising battle and homesteading scenes. We became so caught up in our play that we lost track of time and place. The drama was heated, real, and immediate. Children who were "horses" reared up and neighed loudly while others tried to "calm" them. We sometimes pranced around as a whole herd of horses, tossing our heads, pretending not to understand the other children trying to join our group.

All too often, this playtime was interrupted by the dreaded milk break. In addition to milk at every meal, twice a day we were served another glass of milk. Some children loved it. But most of us hated to see the nurses arrive in the middle of morning or

Susan during first six months

afternoon playtime bearing trays of small glasses. Many years later, at one of the reunions, I asked about the color, which was a deep yellow. I thought something had been added to it make it that color, vitamins perhaps, until a former patient explained it to me. It was pasteurized, not homogenized, milk. We were basically drinking milk with full butterfat in it. I never learned to like it. Most of all, I hated that the milk break signaled the end of our time outside playing and the only time any of us had a moment of freedom from the routine.

5

My Only Friend

Dinner, the largest meal of the day in the South, was always at noon. Whether we were coming from classes or from morning play outside, we all lined up, once again in single file, at the back concrete steps to march into the dining room at midday, finding a spot and waiting to sit down until the director's bell gave the signal. We were served a full, very hearty meal with plenty of vegetables, meat—most often pork or chicken, which was frequently fried for Sunday dinners—a roll or cornbread, and a dessert . . . and more of the dreaded yellow milk. Occasionally, for dessert, we had ice cream, which was a huge treat. Many former patients remember the special coffee-flavored ice cream. Often, we had egg custard, which in my opinion was just another form of yellow milk, with eggs that wobbled in a shallow dish. I found it amazing how many recipes and dishes could be devised for milk and eggs, both of which I hated.

We were expected to eat every morsel. Every one of us, at least once if not more often, ended up remaining at the table to finish our food long after everyone had left for the next activity. We all shared stories of mealtime "prison." After the food had sat for a long time, it was singularly unappetizing, dry, congealed, and cold.

After dinner, we returned to the dorms for an additional "personal hygiene" break. As always, the nurses followed us with clipboards and recorded every action and movement. Then we gathered in the ward to get ready for naptime. There was the sound of low talking as we walked to our assigned beds, climbed in, and lay down. Slowly, complete quiet settled over the room as each girl lay down in her bed.

We were always reminded of the "proper sleeping position": lying on our backs with our arms by our sides, and our heads turned to the front of the room. In theory, this allowed the nurses to efficiently and quickly scan the room to check on us. But it was not a natural position in which to fall asleep.

Upon waking, we took a long walk or had another playtime. Walks took place on the grounds of the Tuberculosis Sanatorium Hospital and Medical Campus, where the preventorium was located. From the front lawn, we could see the long walkway leading down to the circular driveway in front. Off to the left, on the other side of the road, were more beautifully maintained lawns. There was a footbridge over a shallow gully. We could see the grounds of the Mississippi Tuberculosis Sanatorium and often walked there in fair weather. This allowed a few children, whose parents were patients there, an opportunity to see them. The rest of us sat on the ground or steps of the hospital looking out over the lawns. We would giggle, exchange secrets, daydream, and just wait as we so often did at the preventorium.

I am sometimes surprised at what I don't remember. But because I was lost in my own imagination amid the extreme routine, it is no wonder days and weeks have vanished from my memories. What I do remember, I remember intensely and completely in detail.

After supper, we gathered in the Circle Room for story time, singing, or television. Television time was brief and strictly controlled and monitored. We saw what they wanted us to see and heard what they wanted us to hear. And we all saw exactly the same thing at exactly the same time.

When we sat in the Circle Room, we were instructed to sit forward on the edge of our chairs, heads up and both feet flat on the floor. This was to promote good posture.

On Sunday mornings, we attended a nondenominational form of Sunday school in the Circle Room, with Bible verses and stories and hymn singing. I was often perplexed by the songs we sang, particularly the hymns. I remember singing "How Great Thou Art." The line that stood out for me was, "Then sings my soul, My Savior God, to Thee." As I sang, I looked around at other children's faces, not understanding what the words meant. We understood the directions, however, and the director's hand gestures that told us to sing these lyrics more boldly and louder.

Teaching the children songs and hymns was a favorite pastime of the director. We were positioned along one half of the Circle Room: taller, older children on the small chairs, younger and smaller ones sitting on the floor in front of them, cross-legged with hands in laps. The director taught us many songs. As an adult, I sometimes wondered how a singer learned a song in another language, but then realized that we had done exactly that while at the preventorium. We mouthed the words that the director said and then learned to sing along with her, even when we didn't understand the story. Our singing was an activity that particularly charmed visitors.

For holidays, we sang secular songs such as "Easter Parade," "Jingle Bells," "Tea for Two," and "Oh, What a Beautiful Morning." I wanted to get through "Oh, What a Beautiful Morning" as quickly as possible, as it was not my favorite. One little girl whispered that instead of singing "In your Easter bonnet," we should be singing, "In your Easter bloomers." We sang in the mornings, we also sang for visitors while arranged in a semicircle in the Circle room, in one of the classrooms, or on the front steps of the building. We also often recited the Lord's Prayer. I thought God's name was Howard: "Our Father in Heaven, Howard be thy name. . . ."

Back home, I had been accustomed to our Presbyterian church routine, which was formal, educational, intellectual—seemingly remote and unemotional. When the minister in his black robe with black velvet bands down either side of his chest and around the

A daily schedule, slightly varied with the seasons, follows:

Rise	6:30
Personal hygiene	6:30— 6:45
Morning exercises	6:45— 7:00
Breakfast	7:00— 7:45
Personal hygiene	7:45— 8:00
Rest in bed	8:00— 8:30
School	8:30—10:00
Mid-morning milk	10:00—10:15
School	10:15—11:15
Play out of doors	11:15—11:45
Personal hygiene	11:45—12:00
Dinner	12:00— 1:00
Rest in bed	1:00— 3:00
Mid-afternoon milk	3:00— 3:15
Play out of doors	3:15— 4:40
Personal hygiene	4:40— 5:00
Supper	5:00— 6:00
Play and story hour	6:00— 7:30
To bed, summer	8:00
To bed, winter	7:30

(All play is out of doors summer and winter, weather permitting.)

Daily schedule

sleeve ends, stepped to the pulpit, high above us all, and raised his palms in the air, everyone stood, and the entire church was filled with the doxology. The astoundingly loud organ music boomed out, and a large, majestic choir guided the congregants. I secretly loved saying the word "doxology" over and over to myself. It was a mysterious word portending spiritual drama. The hymns we sang at the preventorium were more "Southern Baptist," as my mother described them to one of her friends on a visit. I could not explain it but intuitively understood the difference.

As part of our routine, we learned to pose for photos. When a newspaper needed a story to fill space, the preventorium would often be featured along with a group photograph of the children. From time to time, an article about the benefits of the place was in some local paper. We were publicity props for the benefit of the preventorium. "See how happy the children are while here!" was clearly the intended message being sent to visitors and readers. Perhaps the adults really did think that we were happy and that none of the children were suffering emotionally. Perhaps they needed to believe we were just fine. Perhaps they could not bear any thought other than that we were happy. That was enough for most people reading the articles and seeing the photos. But when I look closely at the pictures, I can tell who is all right and who is miserable.

Although we were locked away at the preventorium, there were few closed doors within. From the double opening of the girls' ward, we could see all the way down the hall into the boys' ward with the row of identical lockers in the middle. The doors were only closed during dressing and bathing hours. Only the front double doors of the building were closed at all times, as was the back door with a wide concrete set of steps leading down into the playground. Inside, all was open, bright, clean, and sterile. We were instead tightly locked away in our routines.

At the preventorium, it was difficult to form close friendships within the strict schedule. It was hard to learn and remember the names of other children as we sat at different places in the dining room every day, and when we filed into single file, we never knew who would be in front or in back of us. Some children often tried to figure out how to get into position close to at least one person she or he knew. A very few children had siblings there, and I envied them as they seemed to be allowed to stay together.

It seemed to me that we existed moment to moment. Perhaps the constant rearranging of children in groups helped to control the large group of children. During only short periods of time when we went outside were we allowed to gather and form friendships. Any other moment that we spent close to another child was snatched while waiting in line in the morning or waiting to line up. These brief communications were heated and often focused on pressing issues like who was disciplined and for what infraction or whom the nurses favored at the moment. The relationships were fervid, stolen, and also could also be brief if one child was to go home. I was fortunate to form one close friendship, but I realized only after I left the preventorium how little I really knew about her, my friend Ethel.

I never knew her last name. Few of us did know each other's last names. I still do not know if I spelled her first name correctly. She was my only real friend at the preventorium. I never had an opportunity to tell her goodbye as my return to home was sudden and unexpected. I always wondered what happened to her.

Not knowing who might leave and when was one of the most difficult realities for us to grapple with. Some children thought that when a child suddenly disappeared, it meant he or she had died. A few sometimes even gathered behind the Brown House during playtime to hold hands and say a prayer for the child who was suddenly gone. I never joined them as it made me think of my father's death.

I understood why they thought the departed children had died. We could all overhear the nurses talking about illnesses, deaths, and patients at the Tuberculosis Sanitorium. It was not an everyday occurrence for a child leave, but when one did go, it happened suddenly, usually during playtime outside. A name would be called to go inside followed a momentary hush as most of the children stopped to watch the child leave then waited to see if he or she reappeared. They might return with a nonscheduled visitor or with a freshly admitted patient.

This was the case with Ethel. She was brought to the preventorium during a playtime one afternoon.

I no longer remember how long I had been at the preventorium when I met Ethel. I do remember that it was late afternoon in a steamy, hot Mississippi summer. I hadn't particularly noticed the heat as we were all acclimated and nearly naked, but I knew it was bad because the nurses and attendants were using ladies' fans, vigorously waving them to generate a breeze. Fans were sometimes ones left on the playground by visitors and sometimes bought from stores in Magee, Mississippi. One featured a picture of an angel in blue and white praying, with the name and address of a funeral home on the back; another was a paper fan that collapsed into a metal rod and clipped shut until needed. I loved fans and always watched whenever anyone used one.

On this particular afternoon, when one of the nurses pulled me aside, I was surprised and a bit annoyed as I had been happily playing out in the wildflower- and weed-strewn fields behind the Brown House and didn't want to leave the playground.

But I stood still and kept my face blank. I knew better than to display my impatience. She was one of the paddle wielding nurses.

"Go inside and meet the new girl," she instructed me. "She's here because her mother has tuberculosis and has to go to the sanatorium—there's nowhere else for her little girl to go except here."

She put her hand on my neck and upper back and gave me a gentle push.

"You are always talking, so you should have no problem making her feel welcome. Go on and be nice. Bring her right back out here to the playground when the nurse says it's okay."

I slowly turned and walked toward the girls' ward, unaware of her implied criticism of my "chattiness," as the nurses called it. I went obediently through the door at the far end of the girls' ward and stopped at the back edge of the double row of lockers, standing quietly so as not make my presence known. The rows of white hospital beds, all made up with white cotton sheets, lining the walls along the windows smelled clean, like the outdoors. I waited and watched from my semihidden spot.

At the entryway to the ward, a group of three adults and one girl about my age—maybe a year or two older—had gathered. She was much taller than I was with sallow skin and very shiny, heavy, black hair done up in a huge round bun at the nape of her neck. On her face was an expression of indescribable sadness, fear, and confusion. She stood very still, looking down at the floor as the adults talked. I watched her hair resting on her neck as she stared down at her feet. She was barefoot and already wearing the preventorium bloomers.

The nurse, in her crisp white uniform, was talking with a couple who also looked sad. Both the man and the woman were dressed in plain clothes that were clearly their best. The man held his black Sunday hat by the brim in his hands and continuously turned it around and around, rolling the edges. I watched him, mesmerized by the turning of the hat brim. The woman was weeping silently, clutching a soaked handkerchief. She kept dabbing at her eyes and snuffling. The nurse was businesslike and brisk. She spoke crisply about the schedule at the preventorium as if they could find some comfort in her "all business all the time" approach.

"She will get used to the routine and be just fine. All the children fall right into line with the daily routine. It will be easy for her."

She stopped and gave the girl an assessing look. "We'll have to cut her hair. I think right now is the best time. She can go to the barber to have it cleaned up the next time he's here," the nurse said. She took a pair of scissors out of her pocket, put her fingers in the handles, and looked speculatively at the girl's head, all the while opening and closing the scissors. She stopped, closed the scissors, and put them back in her pocket and then suddenly declared, "This long hair must be a chore to maintain all the time."

She put her hands on the girl's shoulders and turned her around to take the rubber band and bobby pins out of her hair. I'd never seen such long hair. It tumbled down her back all the way to the floor and trailed a little behind her. It was so black, shiny, and thick. The girl shook her head a little to loosen it.

The nurse took out the scissors again. Suddenly, with one hand, she caught up the hair into sections, each one a thick rope and cut it with just a few snips of the sharp scissors. It only took two or three cuts to get most of the length off. She turned the girl around again and told her to be still while she cut the bangs. The girl now looked like every other little girl at the preventorium. She stood stone still with her head bent toward the floor, mute and unhappy.

The woman, who I learned later was her aunt, bent down and tearfully gathered up the thick pile of hair spilled onto the floor, twisting it into a rope of sorts and putting a rubber band around it. Strands of hair stuck out of the awkward looped bundle.

"Oh, her mother will be so sad," she wailed. "It was such beautiful hair. I'll make her mother a plait to keep and use some for a locket for her to keep with her at the sanatorium."

The girl, her hair now a shiny cap of black, suddenly looked up and saw me. There was a mute pleading in her eyes. She still had said not a word. I remembered my instructions and walked quickly over to the group.

"Hi, I'm Susan." I smiled at her, ignoring the adults. I looked deep into her eyes, which were dark brown, almost black, like her hair, with thick eyelashes and brows.

"Hi, I'm Ethel," she said shyly.

I reached out and took her hand, and we turned away from the adults, walking down the ward, past the beds and lockers, and out the back steps to the playground. We left the uncle with his hat and the aunt, still weeping, holding both the big hunk of hair and her handkerchief in her hands together, the nurse still talking. Ethel never looked back at them.

We became inseparable. I maneuvered my position in line so that we were separated only by one little boy or girl, and or even right next to each other. Our beds were next to each other in the ward. We managed to sit at the same table in the dining room for most meals; although we didn't often get to sit next to each other, we were usually across the table. We would signal each other with our eyes, wriggling our noses and raising and lowering our eyebrows to indicate what we liked or disliked about the meal. Once I tried to reach under the table with my toes to touch her toes by stretching my legs as far as I could, but I ended up sliding underneath the table and getting reprimanded to sit up straight in my chair.

Ethel. Over the years, I've wondered if I made up the spelling of her name.

Ethel was so shy, so uncertain, and always quiet. She stayed by my side all the time. I felt a kinship and a closeness with her that I could not explain. We were strangers in this place where children regularly appeared and disappeared. Ethel and I never talked about what would happen if one of us was suddenly called inside to leave.

I was always struck by how alone we all were in this place. Children were added and subtracted constantly, a moving number between thirty-five and forty, like marbles to a bowl, or constantly newly hatching chicks, all made to look as much the same as possible. There were many more of us than adults, but we were always in single files, following protocol, never daring to be different, at least not where any adult could see us. Ethel and I became close somehow in spite of the isolating routine designed to keep us in control at all times.

Ethel would do anything I suggested. If I wanted to play cowgirls and ride stick ponies, she was right there next to me. If I wanted us to get on the roundabout, go as fast as possible until we dizzily staggered off, giggling and wobbling, falling onto the grass, she was right there with me. She was taller and stronger and could swing even higher than I could.

She never initiated any playground activities but faithfully stayed alongside me at the seesaws, the swings where we would challenge each other to see how high we could go and then drag our feet on the ground to slow ourselves down, or in the Brown House where we wove big cloth loops into potholders to give as gifts.

When outside, Ethel and I also focused on exploring the flowers, trees, and fields as far as we could go while remaining in the official boundaries of the playground. She could identify all the flowers and even the weeds.

"That's dandelion greens," she would point out, plucking one or two to show me. "We gather these up for supper in the spring when they are little and no flowers have bloomed."

She described her mother, grandmother, and aunts going into the woods to search for dandelion greens, wild grapes, sumac, sorrel, and paw-paw, a wild green melon with a custardy yellow interior. I knew paw-paws because my grandmother would carve small ones into little shapes for me: a tiny baby crib, a lantern, or a flower. My cousins, at Sunday afternoon reunions with my mother's family, would tease me by singing a song: "Where's little Susie? Pickin' up paw-paws... way down yonder in the paw-paw patch!" I hated that song, but I loved the tiny carved fruit my grandmother gave me—dark green on the outside, buttery yellow inside—that slowly dried into shriveled shapes a few days later.

Ethel would sometimes surreptitiously pick a flower or a green and pop it in her mouth. I knew she was homesick. Most of the children were terribly homesick all the time. I wondered what was wrong with me that I didn't miss my mother and brother. Was I just numbed to the feelings? I did think of them but did not feel the ache of homesickness. I wanted to observe the world in which I found myself and yet, there was always an underlying sense of uneasiness, an unspoken understanding that life could change dramatically at any moment. I knew there was no safety in this world.

Ethel was my shield, my spiritual communicant, my own special friend. We had no need to talk much, we understood each other's expressions. In many ways, she reminded me of my maternal grandmother, a true southern country woman who could see a dress once, make a pattern and perfectly recreate it, hear a tune and play it immediately on the piano without ever having had a lesson in her life, or make herbal potions to heal any illness her grandchildren had. Like Ethel, she had long dark hair and was silent in a way born of a hardscrabble life in the country. Beauty and pleasure came in small doses to her and to Ethel as well. Her delight in a tiny wildflower or pebble was heartbreaking.

On walks, Ethel was either in front of me or behind me. We would put our hands on our hips and do our "funny" walks, swinging our elbows forward, left elbow, then right elbow. This was easy to do since a nurse or attendant couldn't absolutely tell if it was deliberate. We were masters at signaling each other with our eyes to warn the other of danger.

Only once, I deserted my dear friend. Naps were a part of the rigid daily schedule. I never wanted to sleep. One day, as I lay in bed on a bright afternoon, I looked around for something to relieve my boredom. I discovered that if I lay on my back, I could fashion imaginary people, little puff cloud beings, out of my voluminous white cotton bloomers by scrunching up two small clumps of the voluminous fabric between my thumb and index fingers. I imagined the puffs as little people talking to each other and I began to entertain myself often this way, moving them in conversations with one another.

One afternoon, Ethel, in the bed next to mine, began to do the same. I whispered to her what my people puffs were talking about, and she whispered back to me. Then, I spied the nurse making her rounds coming from the back of the room. Ethel didn't see her as her head was turned to me. The nurse pounced upon her suddenly and slapped her bare leg with an open palm, saying in a low voice, "Go to sleep this instant! Do not cry and waken everyone!"

Ethel's mouth opened into a perfect O, and tears squeezed out silently of her eyes. As soon as I saw the nurse, I pretended to be asleep but watched everything from under my lashes. Ethel assumed I was asleep and told me about what had happened when we were in line for our "personal hygiene" after naptime. Out of guilt, I never told her I had seen the nurse coming or that I had been fascinated by her soundless expression of alarm and fear and how perfectly round her mouth had been. Late at night, when I could not sleep, I thought about my selfishness and vowed to make it up to her by finding a perfect honeysuckle flower. We both loved to press tiny flowers in our school notebooks.

I missed her when we took walks to the Tuberculosis Sanatorium hospital, and she visited her mother. I felt unshielded and exposed without her. The rest of us sat on the steps of the sanatorium hospital. It was more than twice as large as the preventorium, and we were never allowed inside. I never thought to ask Ethel about her father, perhaps because I no longer had one. Our lack of curiosity is now surprising, but we accepted our fates without question.

On the way back to the preventorium, Ethel was always quiet and sometimes silently wept. I did not know how to comfort her except to take her hand when we were back in the Circle Room, getting ready to listen to a story or to sing. Eventually, she would wipe her tears and smile as we sang along to the chosen song.

I often wonder if Ethel ever thinks of me and our time at the preventorium.

I wonder if she found a new friend after I left or if she was lonely. I wished that I had known her full name and was able to find her. She made my time there bearable. I can tell a difference in my demeanor in photos during the time we were friends. I look healthier, happier, and perhaps a little smug about my friendship with her.

One afternoon during naptime, after Ethel and I had been best friends for a while and when neither of us was sleepy, I convinced her to join me in the ultimate adventure—finding the director's closet. This was an example of Ethel's devotion to me. She followed me blindly and without question.

I was obsessed with the director's clothing and shoes, especially since she was one of the few people at the preventorium who wore something other than a uniform. As director, she was VERY busy. We did not see her often except at dinner, Sundays, and the times she joined us in the Circle Room to teach us a new hymn or song. She was very elegant, with a perfect upswept hairstyle, and always wore jewelry, usually pearls. She dressed in tailored, belted shirtdresses or beautifully cut, fitted suits. I loved her shoes the most—high heels, pumps, wedge sandals in summer—all matching her outfit.

Every morning at breakfast in the dining room, I held my breath, waiting to see what the director was wearing. Sometimes it was a freshly pressed, deep navy-blue shirtdress with a crisp, cape-style collar and three-quarter-length sleeves, tightly belted at the waist and with a full-gathered, tea-length skirt. Sometimes it was a smartly cut, pearl-grey suit with the jacket buttoned up and a white Peter-Pan-collared blouse peeking out and a slim, pencil skirt with a kick pleat in the back, accompanied by black, patent-leather, kitten-heeled pumps.

I was convinced her closet must be a wonderland of gorgeous, stylish clothes and shoes.

I was starved for fashion. I missed watching my mother's meticulous routine every morning getting ready for work as she picked out her outfit and shoes to match. I loved the sound of her high heels clicking on our tile floors, sounding so sharp and sophisticated. I was enchanted by the way she got into the car. She would sit sideways on the driver side of the seat and swing her legs, knees held closely together, around and under the steering wheel. I liked watching her shoes swing around to the pedals. She told me this was the proper way for a lady to get into a car.

In those days, all ladies wore, or at least carried, a pair of gloves. I loved watching my mother choose each day among the many pairs of beige, navy, white, and black gloves. She often wore small hats to work, but always wore a fancy hat for church. Her Sunday hats were not ostentatious and usually tastefully small, with a short veil and perhaps a bow, a silk flower, or few tiny feathers. Watching her, I could not wait until I was a grown up and could wear elegant hats, high heels, and gloves. I loved fashion even at a young age.

I knew I must see the closet of wonders—the director's closet.

While I reveled in the freedom of our bloomers, I missed the variety of clothes women wore. I missed going to church and seeing the pretty dresses classmates wore in Sunday School and the funny hats ladies wore in church, some with wide brims and huge feathers that sometimes bumped against family members' heads as they all sat down together in the pew. I missed wearing petticoats. One time I stood at the front of the church for a chil-

dren's program and proudly pulled up my skirt to show the edge
of my red petticoat.

The stairway leading to the director's apartment was close to
the girls' ward, so we caught glimpses of her coming and going
during the day. A wild ambition bloomed and grew within me,
my heart beating hard each morning as I watched the director
descend the stairway from her apartment—first the shoes, then
the clothes, and finally the director herself, poised, hand lightly
resting on the banister as she tapped her way down.

One day, I could wait no longer. I had to see the director's
clothes closet.

It was just after naptime. Everyone was moving about sleepily
in the ward, milling about. Two nurses guided little girls to the
bathrooms. They were talking to each other and not paying much
attention to anything else. The daily routines blurred attention as
every day was the same.

I pulled Ethel to my side, whispering to her to follow me. We
sidled over to a small group of girls. I kept hold of Ethel's wrist
and pulled her gently along with me as we sidestepped past the
lockers, close to the open double doors of the ward.

I almost missed seeing the director turn the corner to go into
the Circle Room, but the flash of her green and white checked
skirt and the click of her high heels caught my attention. I knew
this was the perfect time to sneak up those stairs and find her
closet.

I quickly pulled Ethel along with me, ignoring her whimpers of fear. We reached the steps. I motioned for Ethel to bend
down and crawl up the stairs on hands and knees. I no longer
remember why I thought this was the safest choice. We perhaps
thought that being low to the ground would protect us from
being seen. We crawled up, as quickly as we could, keeping close
to the wall. No one saw us. Still crawling, we discovered the door
to the apartment, slightly ajar so that we could catch a glimpse
into the apartment.

My heart beat rapidly and I paused, wanting to savor the intense pulsing of blood in my ears. Was this freedom and adventure, that felt so close to fear?

The rest of the apartment appeared as a blur to me as we went in, still on hands and knees. It was only the closet I wanted, which was in a room off to our right. I carefully pushed the door open. We crawled into the bedroom. It was an incredibly feminine room with a pink peony flowered quilted bedspread, dust ruffle and curtains to match. The closet had a bright-white, louvered door that was cracked open. I pushed it open wider, sat back on my legs and feet, and looked inside.

There it was, hanger after hanger of dresses of all kinds: suits, shirtdresses, and slim, belted sheath dresses in all manner of pattern and colors. There were shoe racks with perfect high-heeled pumps, sandals, and even a pair of penny loafers, all matched together, the toe of each shoe pointing up on its individual rack. I had barely had a chance to gasp over the beautiful shoes and no chance to study the variety of clothes hanging there when Ethel pulled on my arm.

"We have to leave. I hear someone coming." She was fearful.

We quickly backed out of the closet and out of the apartment on our hands and knees, then crawled into the hall and down the stairway. No one was there. We sat on the bottom stair, breathing hard. Our hands and knees were quite dirty. We could not have been very long in the apartment, perhaps five or ten minutes. Back in the ward, girls were still wandering about, opening and closing their lockers, and lining up for "personal hygiene." The nurses were near the back of the ward. We could hardly believe our luck. By some miracle, no one had seen us. We slipped into the group and lined up with the other girls. I went through a mental snapshot of all that I had seen. In a matter of seconds, I had instinctively memorized the clothes and shoes. Perhaps I invented some as well. Throughout my time at the preventorium, I thought often about that closet, cataloging clothing patterns and designs and counting

Ethel with Susan

different styles of shoes, often while trying to fall asleep. I thought
of it as a secret world of pretty things right above our heads. And
I continued to check the director's shoes every day. I was waiting
to see her wear the penny loafers. She never did.

When we were in the playground, Ethel and I often recited to
each other the kinds of shoes and dresses we had seen:

Stairway to second floor

"SKIRTS with PLEATS," I would shout.

"CHECKS and PLAIDS," Ethel would shout back.

Ethel would have recited anything I requested. She was a dear, sweet, obedient, and humble girl.

6

Fear and Ecstasy in the Night

Every day we took a walk outside along the paths on the medical complex, around the lawns, or to the tuberculosis hospital.

Ethel and I would fall in line together, usually by switching places with whoever was in between us once the nurse's back was turned. It seemed to me that we walked miles and miles. Occasionally, we walked close to the entrance of the medical campus and could see the railroad that ran across the street. I remembered the bump of our car going over the rails on the first day I came to the preventorium. We walked all around the campus, on any sidewalks available, but also through the grass. Our bare feet were always dirty and were the first thing we were told to wash at our evening baths.

"Scrub your face, hands, and feet," nurses ordered us.

Many times, we encountered thorns that we called "stickers." We walked a path next to the preventorium building where they flourished, hidden in the undergrowth of leaves, branches, and grass. And yet the nurses continually led us though this section, again and again, and watched us pull the thorns out of the arches, toes, and heels of our feet.

All of us wondered why we came this way almost every day. During late afternoon walks, we hopped through this thorny patch of branches and leaves. It was an obstacle course of trying to keep up and yet also trying to avoid the pricking thorns hidden in the grassy path.

I had learned to walk on the very outermost edge of my heels, but losing balance every once in a while, I would stumble a bit and a thorn would lodge in the tender part of my arch or between my toes. We all looked like drunken little soldiers, in a straight line, arms akimbo, lurching from side to side to avoid the dreaded stickers. As we came around to the front of the preventorium building, we hurried to sit on the concrete stairs and remove the stickers from our feet while the nurses watched us impassively.

◆ ◆ ◆

Fresh air and a great amount of sleep were key features of life at the preventorium, so we went to bed while it was still daylight or at least twilight in summer. In the winter, we went to bed earlier as it grew dark soon after supper. From the Circle Room, we would walk our robot walk with hands at our waists, girls turning right, boys turning left. Then, our morning rituals were repeated in reverse: brush teeth, put on pajamas, "personal hygiene," with the assigned night nurses taking notes.

Five times a week, before putting on pajamas, we bathed, the littlest ones two at a time in one of the big, elevated tubs, the older girls in the communal shower room. When I first arrived, I was so small that I was a "tub girl," even though I was six. I climbed up a few steps to get into the tub with soapy water. The tubs were filled only a quarter of the way since after each bath, the water would be drained and the tub filled again for the next set of little girls. At some point, I graduated to join the girls in the communal shower. This was great fun as I liked to slide along the walls under the shower heads to see how long I could stay dry. I set myself a goal to slide underneath the twelve shower heads on all four walls without getting soaked. But I never accomplished this because the other girls following along sloshed water over everyone. The nurses did not reprimand us for this silly playing in the water. I don't remember being bothered by anyone's nakedness. No one else seemed to mind or notice either. It was not much different than wearing just bloomers with nothing else on. And on the days when we did not bathe, no one had any shame in dropping their white bloomers, donning pj's, and then marching to bed.

Over time, I accommodated and became just another little girl—a cog in the wheel of the daily routines. The sounds of morning and night became a comforting and familiar low susurration of activity. We were always waiting for the next thing, the next direction, the next place to walk. We did not analyze or ask questions. We followed the schedule. But our minds were our own lands of imaginative opportunity.

Every time we were in bed—whether morning, naptime, or bedtime—I studied the others, the nurses, and the routines. We were always reminded to get into the "proper" sleeping position. If we turned over at any time while sleeping, some nurses would reposition us, turning us onto our backs. Others would wake us to get on our backs. Some children woke to a paddle slapping their thighs to make them remember to sleep on their backs. I was often awake in the night and saw the kinder nurses bending over beds, adjusting arms and heads so they were aligned with all the other children in the ward.

As the days and weeks moved into months, I moved around the ward to new beds in various locations. We all shifted to a different place as new little girls arrived. Our movements, always to the right, were a balletic grand jeté from bed to bed around the long ward.

My first bed was located near the nurses' station. I was not in the first bed but the third. The first two were not occupied. Over the months, I shifted to the next bed and then the next, until eventually, I found myself in the first bed on the left of the ward. No one ever questioned this. For some of us, it was a way to mark time in a place where there was no time. We counted down how many days we might sleep in a specific bed.

Our days seemed endless. Tall girls, small girls, each moving in the same synchronized patterns and rhythms every morning and every night. Was I the only one who saw hundreds of blurred images from the past to the present, following the same steps and routines? I lay in my bed and saw the ghosts of thousands of girls over the years, filling the ward, marching from the dining hall, lining up for teeth brushing, face washing, lockers, and pajamas.

In the day, the ward was a haven, safe and warm with sunlight pouring in. I often pretended to sleep at naptime and eventually did fall asleep. But first, I always surreptitiously studied the expressions of the other little girls. What were they dreaming about? What was in their heads? We all traveled to another world in our sleep, and I found that fascinating.

Each night, through the enormous windows, which were lifted to the ceiling in the summer to let the heat out and the cool night air in, I lay in bed and watched the sky darken and turn to night. The nights, unfettered from routine, became both my time of terror and my mind's playground. Once the nurse had finished her rounds and sat down at her station, I began my nightly thinking and observation.

First, I studied the pattern of my pajamas. I had three pairs made by my maternal grandmother. My very favorite ones had an aqua background with circles of tiny boys and girls in Bavarian or Swedish folk dress dancing in a circle. I spent hours at night studying the little girls with yellow braids, their aprons embroidered with roses, and the boys in hats with feathers and in lederhosen embroidered to match the girls' aprons. They were all in clogs and smiling with joined hands. Round and round they danced in folk dances. I imagined them roaming the countryside at night with brightly lit campfires and singing, free to wander wherever they wanted. Often, I bunched the fabric up so that the little circles were raised and then twisted the fabric back and forth to make the dancers move.

For more than four hundred nights at the preventorium, I did not clearly see the stars or moon. We went to bed early—8:00 p.m. in the spring and summer during sunset, 7:30 p.m. in the fall and winter. If I stared long enough out the window and the screens were not pulled tight, I might see part of the moon or a star through the branches of the trees, unless it was my mind conjuring them up.

The ward at night was mysterious, sometimes dramatically romantic with shadows from the moonlight, or devilishly frightening in the utter darkness of cloudy nights. Girls who looked normal in the daylight became ghoulish and pale lying on their backs, heads and faces turned in the same direction, eyes closed. Moans or whimpers escaped them periodically. Sitting up in the bed when the nurse was not looking, I could peer down the entire row of little girls in the beds, pale ghouls all eerily seeming to stare at me, even with their eyes closed, as they all had their heads turned toward me.

Sometimes, I was not sure if the nurses were real in the dark. Sleeping girls were left alone, so I always pretended to be asleep.

Lying in the stark white bed at night, unable to sleep, and looking out the huge windows, I mentally created a different world—especially when there was moonlight. The moon sent great shafts of silvered light through the windows into the spaces that fell between the beds. Sometimes the shafts of light overlapped with the beds, and a girl might lie half in moonlight and half in darkness.

I imagined the huge shafts of light beaming into the room as light filled hallways to the treetops—to worlds, whirling in the sky, lifting me up and away. I longed for a prism to hold close to my eyes, one that would reveal the hallways of light. I was sure that I could transport myself deeper into those moonlit hallways and walk into a beautiful, faraway, silvery world. But I was alone in a room of sleeping girls in pristine white beds. I was awake in a room of sleepers with hallways of light I could not enter.

Night was unknowable and mystical, but it was also the time of my greatest fears. I was terrified of the darkness that collected in the corners of the rooms beyond the ward, of the unknown world beyond the windows, of the darkness of the hallway behind the nurse's station, and especially of the darkness and suffocation of my own closed eyes as I tried to go to sleep. The black dark of night was overwhelming.

At some point, I was moved to a bed in front of the last window facing the front lawn and near the semicircular toy room where I lay awake paralyzed and feverish with fear. The two empty beds next to the toy room loomed large, and the bed linens gleamed with a sullen, white glow. The Cross of Lorraine on the coverlet darkened to black in the night. I knew I was nearest the danger zone of whatever horrors might creep out of the toy room and into the ward. I was convinced that the menacing stuffed toys, on shelves along the walls, were moving toward me. I could see them opening their glassy eyes at night, staring at me alone in the bed.

The nurse was gone for a break or perhaps asleep as well—or, in my worst imaginings, gone forever to leave us in the terrible black night with toys moving in the dark room next to me. I was too terrified to move. If I lay as still as possible, perhaps I would escape notice. But I could feel the toy animals shifting in the dark, whispering and plotting. I tried not to look, but it was impossible. I kept turning my head and opening my eyes to peer into the darkness. I was certain they stopped moving when they saw me looking at them. And what lay on the other side of the door to the playground? I heard monsters on the swings and seesaws. I saw gaping holes in the earth, swallowing up the preventorium ward where I lay. On most nights, I pretended to be asleep when the night nurse passed on her rounds, but this night, paralyzed with fear, I prayed for her to come to check on me.

I had learned that people could disappear suddenly without explanation, like my father, like me being left here, like children leaving and never returning and now, like the nurse disappearing into the dark hall. I wondered if she was gone forever like others.

Late one night as I lay staring into the corners of the room for emerging monsters, I could feel transference from the sheets and bed frame. They were communicating with me. They told me their history, how the sheets had been handled by the people who made them. I could absorb the sunlight directly from the freshly laundered sheets that had been dried outside, hanging on a line in the hot sun. I could feel the cool wooden shelf the sheets had lain on once folded. I could see the iron pieces of the bed frames being forged. I could sense the metal cooling and feel the iron of the bed frame as it was put together, holes matched up, screws turned tightly, the bars in the headboard wiped of dust. I felt the weight of the sheets and blanket in the winter. Once I sneaked out of bed and took a Cross of Lorraine coverlet to put over myself in bed. I wanted to feel the heaviness of the fabric, the depth of the blood-red double cross, symbol of death to so many. I thought of my father and waited to die in the blackness of night to join him. But I didn't.

In the midst of my fear, I always felt on the edge of chaos, even though I did not know the word. At any moment, my smile would crack around my entire head so that the top of my head opened up. My arms would fall off at the shoulder and stick to my waist where my hands gripped my sides for walking in single file. Blood would pour from my head and shoulders. I would remain standing, fixed, a blood fountain. I imagined the horror that would ensue, much running of various nurses, a mop and pail produced while I spouted blood as red as the Cross of Lorraine.

In my childhood memory of nights at the preventorium, it was always moonlit with the pine trees dropping cones that made noises that sounded like muffled footsteps coming toward me. Sometimes as moonlight fell in shafts between the branches, they created parallelograms on the ground. These trees, spread throughout the lawns, that looked so expansive and peaceful during the day became a pathway to terror at night. I could see them, the trees, in the night through the tall windows in the girl's ward—windows with no shades, no covering. There were inner shutters, but I do not remember them ever being closed.

A few times in the night when I was frightened, I called out to the girl in the next bed in a low voice to wake up, but she never did.

Was she not afraid of the dark or was I, closest to the monstrous room, her protection? Was I designated the sacrificial offering to whatever lurked there? I sometimes was so terrified that I would fall into a state of fearful ecstasy like the religious figures we had learned about in Sunday School lessons. The mind, the body can sustain terror only so long before passing into a semiconscious state of watchful stillness. Once, in a heated state of fear, time stood still. I stared at a corner of the ceiling, trembling, and saw a tiny speck of light emerge and slowly grow. The light flowed from the far corner of the toy storage room. In my misery, I watched the light, rimmed with pink-gold billowing edges grow and surround me. My fear began to flow away, and my body relaxed involuntarily. Surely this was an angel, like the ones in the pictures from Sunday School, sent to soothe me. Or perhaps it was a Greek or Roman goddess from my Greek myth storybooks. Was it Diana coming from the moon to guide me through the dark? My body relaxed; my eyes closed in exhaustion. I felt peace flow through my body as I drifted to sleep, the golden pink light with the glowing edges imprinted on my inner eyelids.

Every night after that, until I was moved to another bed, I closed my eyes and pictured the rosy glow around me, a blanket of safety in the night. I waited for the feeling of fear to turn to peace, oozing throughout my fevered brain.

During the day, the light was bright and cheerful, almost dazzling. In the heat of the summer, there was little noise except for the occasional swoosh of birds flying. Once, very late in the afternoon, near sunset, we all ran to the windows to exclaim over a huge flock of birds swelling up and down, swooping in big circles before settling into the trees. Later in the classroom, we learned this was a "murmuration." I loved saying the word over and over to myself. Sometimes as I lay in bed, walked in line, or sat in the classroom, I repeated the word as a self-soothing chant. Mentally, I varied the syllable accent to change the word, remembering the swooping and dipping of the birds, seemingly random but with a carefully synchronized rhythm. Our teacher told us the birds flocked together for safety and helped each other learn to stay together. This meant they were good at following rules, just like us.

Although I never said so, I no longer trusted God, who had taken my father from us and allowed me to be here. I loved the colorful Bible stories, the drama of the stigmata of the crucifixion, the stone rolled away from the grave, the blessings of Jesus, and the wrath displayed in the Old Testament, but I did not love God as I was told to do in Sunday School. I went along with everyone and sang the hymns and prayed, or at least pretended to pray. I thought about the comforting glow I had seen and how I would rather pray to one of the powerful and dramatic Greek or Roman gods than to a cold, remote, and selfish God who stole loved ones away with such abrupt ferocity.

◆ ◆ ◆

Until Ethel came to the preventorium, the nights were long even with my self-soothing methods of touching my lip and picturing the soft glow of clouds surrounding me. But once she was there, we figured out a way to keep our beds next to each other where the windows faced the playground. We could see part of the Brown House, where toys were kept for outside play.

Other girls also maneuvered to sleep next to each other. Two younger girls even managed to crawl into bed with each other for several nights. Luckily for them, the nurse on duty was kind enough to pick one up and move her back to her bed, but when it happened two or three more times, she told them it had to stop or they would get into trouble. They were very lucky not to have been paddled in the night, or worse, humiliated in front of everyone.

Throughout the time I was there, I thought about how some children were treated better than others. All of us were well aware of the differences in treatment by nurses and staff. I wondered if anyone felt really safe within the routinized life we led. Even though the nurses seemed to believe in the health benefits of the routine, it seemed to all of us that it was mainly used to control us.

On the first day of the preventorium's existence, were the children surprised when they awoke? Did it feel brand new to them? I hadn't had time to be surprised the first morning after my arrival; I had to jump right into a strange new routine. I asked Ethel if she was surprised her first morning, but she said she was just scared at being away from her mother and her home.

"What if," I asked her as we stood in line to brush our teeth, "we moved the beds at night, so that people go to sleep in one place and then wake up in a different place? If someone goes to sleep facing the wall and then wakes up in front of a window, will it be a surprise or a fright or nothing at all? Will they notice if they wake up next to a new person?"

Ethel asked why I cared and said she didn't understand. I was convinced we had to test this. I needed to see the faces of the girls after we moved of their beds. In fact, I was compelled to discover this. So, at night, while trying to fall asleep, I laid out a plan.

We would quietly get out of bed and then move the beds on either side of us so they were switched with one another. This meant unlocking the caster wheels on each hospital bed. During the day, I sat on the floor tying my sneakers slowly so I could examine the wheels. Each bed had four, rubber-tired wheels with locks that could be loosened. Over several days, I studied the wheels, the bed locations, and the distance from the nurse's station.

Ethel's and my beds were in the middle of the ward, mine against a window, Ethel's against a wall between windows. We were on the same side as the bathrooms and shower room.

Finally, I was ready. We were shielded from the night nurse's view by the lockers. To see us, she had to walk around the entire ward, which she did several times a night to check for sleeping positions, etc. I waited until the nurse had walked past us and slowly rose so that I could peer over the lockers to watch her. She picked up a clipboard at the nurse's station and walked out into the hall and disappeared.

I woke Ethel up to get her to help me move the beds. She was sleepy and at first didn't want to get up, but I kept shaking her and asking her to help. She was much taller than me and when we hugged, she could put her chin on the top of my head. I needed her strength. She stood sleepily with her arms wrapped around herself, watching me.

"Here," I whispered, "help me undo the wheels. We have to be quiet and fast."

The beds were heavier than I expected, and I was surprised at how awkward it was to move them. I had envisioned them wheeling quietly and quickly. Looking at photos of the ward, I'm surprised we could move them at all, but we did. Slowly, slowly, so as not to wake the sleeper, we switched two beds and then another two.

"Let's move ours too so we can be surprised when we wake up," I whispered delightedly.

We must have taken longer than we thought because the night nurse came back, astonished to see us up. She didn't seem to notice the order of the sleeping girls had changed but saw us moving our own beds. She was aghast.

"What do you think you are doing?" she hissed furiously at us. "Stop that this minute."

She grasped each of us by the upper arm, squeezing hard, and dragged us to the bathroom and shower. Ethel was whimpering, and I was trying to keep up.

She marched us into the shower room and stood us in opposite dark corners of the room. It was a square room with tiled walls and floors, and shower heads set at intervals. It seemed huge, an endless dark void in the night with no windows. We could only see the doorway, where the faint white of the washroom lavatories and tubs gleamed.

I kept my eyes focused on the faint light in the rectangle of the doorway. I could hear Ethel snuffling and whimpering in her corner.

After what seemed an eternity, the nurse came back to check on us. I was sure she had a paddle, and I quickly scooted along the wall, turning on every shower head I could. She would have to walk through pouring water to reach us. I had turned on two showers when the nurse appeared framed in the pale light of the doorway. We both froze in place.

To my utter surprise, the nurse stood in the doorway and laughed. She beckoned with her finger for us to come out of the shower room. Ethel rushed to the doorway, wanting nothing more than to return to the safety of her bed. I reluctantly followed her. We both stood anxiously just outside the door of the shower room. I was very damp from being underneath the showers.

"Girls, if you will go back to bed and just go to sleep, you won't be punished."

She smiled at us and whispered, "I mean it. You both need to be in bed. Go turn those showers off and come back out here."

I slid along the tiled walls, feeling the coldness of wet tile as I turned off all the showers. The nurse brought us dry pajamas from our lockers. I could see one or two girls in beds shifting in their beds at the unexpected sounds, but none awoke.

We pulled on dry pajamas and went to our beds, climbed in, and lay on our backs, heads turned in the right direction. Once the nurse was gone, we looked at each other and giggled at our adventure and the near miss with the paddle. Ethel fell asleep quickly. I watched, as always, with my eyes almost closed but not quite, as the nurse made rounds of the ward. The next thing I knew, it was morning.

Later that next day on the playground, I heard the nurse telling another nurse that our adventure had livened up the usually tedious night shift. But after that, she never left the ward until she was certain that we were fast asleep, even though I often tried to wait her out.

And that morning, no one—not one single girl—uttered a peep about having gone to sleep in one location and woken up in

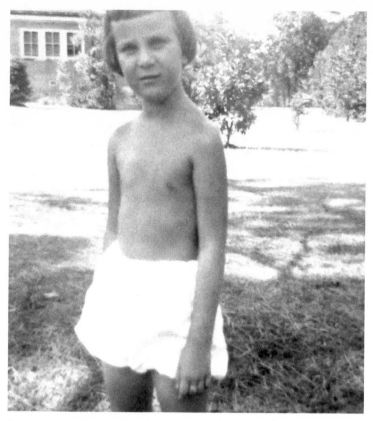

Susan, pensive on a hot afternoon

another. Either I had not made a dramatic enough change, or they just blindly accepted whatever happened in the preventorium. Or was it that no one dared to ask about a bed moving? The nurse told my mother on a Sunday visit, and they had a good laugh about it, although my mother cautioned me to behave.

I sometimes thought about trying the experiment again but never did.

On long, hazy afternoons, drowsy in the heat, I wondered if ghosts of those who were here before us haunted the preventorium. I watched for them—the ghosts of the endless little girls who had come before me, rising, dressing in the bright glare of the ward, white everywhere, with the blazing lights overhead and the sun streaming through the windows. I saw the blur of little ghost girls rushing to jump into beds, open lockers, line up in single file.

I knew that space so intimately, every dust mote, every piece of furniture, every square of the shiny linoleum, every leg of every hospital bed. Never again would I know a place so completely. I knew every crack in the ceilings, every loose knob on a cupboard, every silent opening of a door. I secretly believed I owned the ward, especially at night, in the dark, when I was the only girl awake. There were no surprises, no mysteries, and no changes to be found, other than the shifting faces of the girls who came and went without explanation.

◆ ◆ ◆

Big and Littles every night,
Big and Littles in my sight.

"Big and Littles" is what I called one of my recurring dreams. I often repeated this refrain to myself as I lay in bed waiting to sleep and to dream. My dreams took me away from my body and myself and into the upper spaces of the rooms. They allowed me to escape the daily drudgery and to roam at will.

Squeezing my eyes tight against the terrifying, sudden darkness of the lights being turned out, I waited and then briefly opened my eyes. It was so dark I could not see anything, even my hand. I felt that I was suffocating in it. I squeezed my eyes so tightly that I felt my cheeks rise up to meet my eyebrows. Then, I sensed myself rising to the ceiling—or was it just my head growing larger and larger until it filled the room?

From my enormous head, up high near the ceiling, I could look down on everyone: tiny, sleeping girls in white beds. I was so big and everyone else so little. "Big and Littles," I thought to myself.

I turned my head back and forth, watching the night nurse at her station, a small lamp casting light over her hand poised on a notebook, her head moving as she read charts. I looked toward the back of the ward at the half-circular room with toys, checking to be sure no toys were moving. Then, turning again, I had to bow my head a little to look out the enormous windows, which took up at least half the space between ceiling and floor. With my gigantic head, I felt the heat rise in the summer, collecting along the ceiling and drifting out the windows. My head continued to grow larger as I felt it expand to encompass the entire ward. It became so huge I couldn't turn it easily. If it was reflected in a mirror, I would only see one side—one eye, one cheek, half my mouth. Where was the rest of my body?

During the long night, I felt myself floating at times, rising to the center of the ceiling, gazing down on the rows of lockers dividing the ward. I could see everyone trying to stay on their backs with arms down by their sides and heads turned, but some were shifting restlessly. I could see my own body in the bed near the back, my head turned fearfully toward the dark, semicircular toy room. I wondered about drifting out the window, through the tiny open sections of the screens. If I could be big, I could also become small enough to escape through any opening. I saw myself floating over the fields we ran through at playtime. I imagined animals, not threatened by any humans, wandering happily and freely through the brush and trees.

Turning my attention back to the ward, I floated through the double doors, down the hallway and into the Circle Room where, from the ceiling, I saw tiny chairs set out around the room, awaiting a singing lesson, or for children to be displayed in a photo session extolling the benefits of the preventorium.

In one waking dream, I floated out of the Circle Room and out the back door, over the steep concrete steps leading down to the playgrounds. I hovered aloft over the swings and seesaws, the bare, hard-packed dirt underneath. On hot days, dust flew about during playtime. I remained there, waiting calmly for something I could not name. The horizon above the trees was lighter than the dark night sky, rising above it as if a thin cloud lay upon the treetops.

Without realizing it, I found myself back inside the hallway with the dining room on my left, the doors open to reveal tables set with crisp white tablecloths and pressed napkins in rings, each place set with heavy white plates, the chairs pushed underneath the tables. It was dark, yet the white table linens reflected light back into the room.

Floating across the hall and into the classrooms, I ended up next to a window where I peered out into the dark fields that were our playgrounds during the day. Tall grass and milkweed swayed in the wind; dark shapes waved across the horizon.

Many nights were spent in dreams such as these, never straying far but carefully and silently surveilling my environment.

Waking from these dreams, and to anchor myself in the real world, I lay in my bed, mentally picturing the children and adults that I saw every day in the preventorium. I know now that I was disassociating to cope with my fear of the night and darkness.

In my dream state, I was confident that I could tap into and share in the collective consciousness of everyone. I could discern every emotion, every thought of the people with whom I shared so much and yet so little.

7

The Crux of the Matter

My father died when I was four. We had been a happy family, my father making us all laugh, my mother's face lighting up, beautiful and devoted whenever he came into the room.

My brother and I have the happiest memories of our life on Sewanee Drive in our little house with a big backyard. We were rambunctious and cheerfully unaware of anything except having fun, especially with our dog, Tippy—a beautiful black-and-white border collie named for the white tip on the end of her tail. Our world was mostly contained to the small two-bedroom cottage, our yard, and immediate neighbors' yards. Ned, my brother, and I were particularly imaginative in making up games together. Once we were in the "Wild West" with my brother, one of his friends, and me, all of us running around the backyard with cowboy boots, hats, and toy holsters. My mother worried a bit (after all, it was the fifties) about a little girl having a holster, but my father said, "Why shouldn't she get to be a cowgirl doing everything her brother gets to do?" He bought me a beautiful cowboy hat that had a pattern like a palomino horse. Once, when my brother and I were imagining that we were in *The Roy Rogers Show*, playing "shoot-'em up at the old saloon," Ned instructed me to go inside the house to be a lookout. I stood by the bedroom window surveilling the backyard. Ned and his friend were nowhere to be found. I grew bored standing there but still had my toy gun in my hand.

Suddenly, Ned's friend ran past the window. Without hesitation, I took the butt of the gun and cracked it against the window. Glass shattered. I stuck my hand out the opening.

"Bang, bang—gotcha, you thieving varmint," I shouted at the little boy, who, along with Ned, had stopped, motionless, in front of the window with his mouth open.

"You are gonna be in so much trouble," Ned said, somewhat nervously and, I thought, a bit happy sounding, too. "Just wait till mama and daddy get home."

We stopped playing for the afternoon. A feeling of dread came over us as we waited for our parents to get home from work. Mary, our sitter, said nothing but kept making a noise that sounded like "emph, emph, emph."

Finally, our parents came home. They had no sooner walked in the front door when Ned blurted, "We were playing cowboys, and Susan broke the window!"

In the flurry of hellos, putting down handbags, papers, keys, and other things, my father said, "Let's go take a look."

All of us trooped into the small bedroom. He crouched down to look at the broken windowpane. "No one was hurt, right?" he asked. We shook our heads no.

"Well, how smart you are to think so quickly—what good reflexes you have," he said as he scooped me up into his arms. He turned to my mother. "Don't we have smart children?" They laughed and later had the window repaired.

He was like that, my father, always seeing the bigger picture.

Once, when I was about three and a half, I was in my bedroom coloring—fast and furiously, intensely, watching colors magically appear on the paper. After a while, I ran out of pages. I stood, clutching my fists full of crayons, looking around the room. I had so many colors yet to use—they begged for a surface on which to be displayed. As I looked around, my eyes rested on the back of the bedroom door. What an enormous space, perfectly blank and square, just waiting for my art. I took a blue crayon and tentatively made a tiny little mark in a corner of the square panel. The color was bright, and it looked perfect. Soon, the entire back of the door was covered in a multitude of colors. It had been a delightful opportunity to use every single color in the 148-crayon box. Some of the names I couldn't even pronounce or read, but I loved how they looked. I lost track of time creating my masterpiece. When our sitter, Mary, came to check on me, she opened the door and saw me with crayons in each hand. She stepped further into the room and saw the back of the door. She clapped both hands onto her cheeks and gasped, "Your mama and daddy gonna be so mad with you. Come outta this room this minute. You gonna sit with me the rest of the afternoon."

I don't remember the rest of that afternoon or when my parents arrived home from work. I do remember my father taking me into the room, looking over the door and turning to me to ask, "Who did this to the door?" He didn't sound very angry at all. I thought for a minute.

"Tippy," I said. Tippy, our sweet, calm border collie, who always kept close to my brother and me.

My father exclaimed, "Tippy? Why how in the world did she manage to do this? How did she manage to hold the crayons and get all of this done?"

"Well," I replied, "she put the crayons in her teeth and put her paws up on the door so she could color."

I demonstrated by putting my hands on the door, a crayon in my mouth, moving my head up and down and side to side.

My father shook his head, saying, "Well, I have never seen such a smart dog!" He called my mother, "Nell, come here and look at what Tippy has done." My mother gasped when she saw the door.

I stood by, smiling proudly as they exclaimed over Tippy's work, talking about how she was the smartest dog ever. This went on for a few days. My father, who was very social, brought neighbors and friends into the room to show them Tippy's art. Everyone exclaimed and agreed that Tippy was indeed a very smart dog.

On Saturday, at breakfast, my father said to my Uncle Jimmy, his younger brother who was visiting, "Jim, we have to talk about Tippy. If she can color the back of the bedroom door, who knows what else she can do? I'm worried about having a dog that smart in the house when we aren't home. I think she might have to go."

"No, no, Daddy, it was me!" I cried out, "I did it! Don't take Tippy!"

My father looked at me with a look of astonishment.

"It was you? You told a fib? To me?"

I burst into tears at the thought of disappointing him. But he picked me up and held me tight, saying there was no punishment forthcoming. He figured the fear of losing Tippy and disappointing him was enough. Later, I sat on the floor as he cleaned and repainted the back of the bedroom door.

This was one of my mother's favorite stories to tell when she talked about my father.

My mother was a different person when she was around him, smiling, sparkling with happiness and delight. She loved every moment of our family time and delighted in dressing my brother and me up for church for photos or just for the fun of it.

Another precious memory of my father took place one day while we drove home from Sunday School and the weekly sermon at Central Presbyterian Church. My parents were chatting in the front seat, while Ned, next to me on the back seat was reading a book. I was gazing out the car window to my left when we stopped at a traffic light.

In the back of the car next to us, I saw the heads of two children, while in front, a man and a woman were talking. The woman turned her head around to talk to the children, and I could see dark, short, curled hair and a small, deep blue velvet hat with black netting. As she spoke, she put her white gloved hand on the back of the car seat.

With a shock of recognition, I saw that they were a family just like us: two parents, a little boy, and a little girl. I looked around our car to confirm and compare. They were so near, so immediate and intimately close to us, I felt they could be in our car with us. I was acutely aware of our existence in our car, my separateness from them as I watched their lips moving and the expressions on their faces. I suddenly had a warped sense of space. As I studied them, I felt so close to the family that I became convinced that I understood them and could participate in their lives. Why couldn't I hear and be present with them, too? Why was I prohibited from sharing in their thoughts? Why did we exist only on one level of consciousness? Why couldn't I hear and be present in that car as well as ours? I did not use those adult words, but I remember pondering this.

"Why are we only in this place?" I asked my parents as I studied the people in the car next to ours. "Why can't we hear other people when we can see them? Why can't we hear each other's thoughts? I can hear them in my head."

It seemed to me we should all be intimately connected somehow, but I couldn't explain or understand what I was trying to ask.

My mother turned around to look at me with a puzzled look on her face. My father, gazing straight ahead while driving simply said, "Ah. You are imagining what they are saying to each other. It's a complicated thing but we can only be in one place at a time and hear only what is near us. We cannot hear others in different rooms or know what anyone is thinking. That is the way the world was designed. We may want to be present with everyone all the time, but it is not possible. "

I wanted to ask why, but then he asked if we wanted to have ice cream, and I forgot my question.

Throughout my stay at the preventorium, I had a fractured sense of time and place. I often wished I had the ability to move through time; to observe myself objectively; to see how and if I fit into the world; to see myself at the preventorium, on the playground, in bed at night. I wished I could see what was happening at home and what might be taking place far from this enclosed world.

There was a stark contrast between being at home one day, in my backyard, or in my small bedroom with dolls and stuffed animals, playing with my brother and Tippy, and then finding myself in this enormous, palatial building with columns and vast lawns.

We moved to a modest three-bedroom ranch house in a new development of South Jackson in 1958. It was after the death of my father, but I don't remember leaving the house on Sewanee Drive, the packing, any people—neighbors or visitors—nothing.

While I have some very happy memories of the time before my father's death, I have very few memories of the eighteen months after my father died suddenly from cardiac arrest due to an overdose of anesthesia. He was in the hospital for a routine procedure, a bronchoscopy. His death at age twenty-seven was a severe and deep shock to everyone, especially for my mother, who adored him. His death changed everything.

My brother, who was six at the time, has clearer memories of our being called into the living room of the tiny two-bedroom cottage on Sewanee Drive that our parents rented.

The house was small: two bedrooms separated by a bathroom, a small living room, a dining room, and a fairly large kitchen. It was a nondescript house, meant to be temporary by my parents. Then all hell broke loose for my mother when my father died unexpectedly.

We had been playing outside in the backyard, Ned told me, and we reluctantly came inside into the small living room. The minister of our church, a kind and brilliant man, was with her. He drew Ned to him for a hug, bending over to wrap his arms around Ned.

We waited anxiously, wondering what was happening and sitting on the floor in front of the couch with our knees together and legs splayed out on either side, in an M shape. Our mother was always trying to change this habit saying, "That will make you knock-kneed."

But that day, she didn't correct us. She sat silently on the edge of the dark brown sofa, twisting a handkerchief in her hands, her eyes big and dark, staring out in the distance. All of a sudden, our mother, still sitting on the couch looked at us and said, "Daddy's not coming home from the hospital. There's been an accident. I'm so sorry." She put the handkerchief to her eyes but immediately pulled it down and started twisting it in her hands again. I was riveted by her hand motion, the way she twisted the small white square one way over her index finger on one hand and then over the index finger of the other.

I didn't really understand what she was saying. The deep sadness in her face and her trembling lips told me that something very wrong had happened. I began to cry because I had heard the "not coming home" part. Ned, confused, asked why our father wasn't coming home.

"There was an accident," she said again, her voice trembling, "and he died." With that, she put her face in her hands and began to weep silently, her entire body shaking.

Ned and I looked at each other, stunned. We understood that he was never coming home again. We began to wail loudly, waiting for our mother to comfort us, but she only wept harder when she saw us crying. The three of us wept for what seemed forever before the minister sat down next to my mother, took both her hands in his, helped her stand up and guided her out of the room, leaving us alone.

In the days after, our house was filled with visitors, people sitting on chairs or standing around in small groups of two or three, talking in low voices. The table in our small dining room was laden with covered casseroles, bread, pies, and cakes, some wrapped in checked or flowered cotton cloths. There was always a church lady, walking around with a percolator coffee pot and offering coffee to people.

A friend of my mother's, a woman in a dark suit, sat with us on the couch and tried to soothe us. She told us that our daddy had gone to heaven, that he was with God, and that we should be happy that he had gone to a "better" place.

"God loved him so much, he took him to his home," she said, smiling at us.

I asked why God would take my father from our happy family. I could not understand her saying that it was a good thing. I knew that something irrevocable had happened, that I would never see my father again, and that nothing would ever be the same. I decided I was angry with God forever.

I left and went to stand in the doorway of my parents' bedroom, watching and listening as people came and left. Whenever I went into the living room, one or another of the adults always smiled at me and called me over to sit on their lap or next to them. They avoided any mention of my father. Once, sitting between a man and woman, I asked them, "Did you know my father died? He's never coming home again." They looked over my head at each other.

"Yes, honey, we are so sorry," the woman said. "But you'll have to be brave for your mama now." I slid off the couch and went into my bedroom.

Sometimes, I went outside to the backyard and sat on a swing, twisting around and watching the chain wind together and then unwind, first one way and then the other. But most of the time, I hid in my father's closet, where his suits still hung and his shoes were paired on a shoe rack. I stayed crouched there as my mother talked with visitors in the living room. I vividly remember hiding in that closet and sitting at meals in the kitchen with my brother and my mother with her dark-rimmed, tired eyes.

When I hid in my father's closet, I put my hands in every pocket of his clothing—suits, trousers, shirts—and was I delighted to find that men's suit jackets had a secret inside pocket on the left side. I found odds and ends: coins, gum wrappers, and the occasional stub from a parking lot, but not much else. I spent many hours sitting on the floor of his closet, behind the shoe rack, the door slightly ajar, the suits and shirts above me. Sometimes, I ran my hands over the bottoms of the clothes to tickle my palms. Also, I rubbed the shiny and smooth toe end of his shoes. Once, I put my hands in his pants pockets and found a pair of cufflinks. I have them still. They are gold with a white porcelain surface, each with a tiny, painted, old-fashioned steamboat, a huge plume of smoke trailing overhead, the paddle and trim of the boat red. I kept them for years before finally putting them in a French cuffed blouse to wear. For all the years I kept them, I never told my mother; now I cannot.

My father was much loved. A handsome and intelligent man, he was born in 1929, in Monticello, Mississippi, a tiny town in the southern half of the state. His family was considered well-to-do; his father was a doctor. He went to Millsaps College in Jackson and was popular and very witty.

Another vivid and happy memory of my father when we lived on Sewanee Drive was the time he hid the platter of barbecued chicken on the shelf of his closet when a neighbor, who had a habit of coming to visit us at mealtimes, showed up at the front door. Not wanting to be rude—but wanting to enjoy a family meal—he hid the platter of chicken he had just taken off the grill on a shelf in a bedroom closet and went to the door.

My brother, and I not understanding, went into the living room and asked, "Daddy, we want some of that chicken that's in your closet."

Without missing a beat, he stood up and laughed, "Is there chicken in the closet? Let's go see."

He stood up, took our hands, one on each side of him and we all, including the unexpected guest, trooped into the bedroom.

He stopped in front of the closet door, held up a hand and said, "Do you think there is really chicken in here? Let me conjure it up in my head."

He closed his eyes and put his hand on the door, appearing to think intently. We were all mesmerized. He stepped back, opened the door with a dramatic swoosh and said, "Well, we do have a platter of barbecued chicken on the shelf here! Just like magic!"

We all applauded, even the nosy neighbor, who was as captivated by our father's performance as we were. We trotted happily after my father as he took the platter down and into the dining room. The neighbor ended up staying for dinner once again and joined in the laughter as my father recounted to my mother how he "conjured up" the barbecued chicken in the closet. He was always confident, ready to laugh, and never unkind. I sometimes wonder if it is better to always remember him as eternally young and happy.

In the aftermath of my father's death, I heard the low murmur of visitors' voices in the living room and the dulled, muted sound of the TV. I knew our mother was sitting on the couch, smoking and gazing into the distance. I have few memories of that time other than sadness. I was happy we moved away from Sewanee Drive.

For a short while before entering the preventorium, I lived in our new house, but most of my memories of my fifth year of life are of St. Dominic's Hospital where I was treated for asthma, asthmatic bronchitis, and pneumonia. A wonderful, kind nun, Sister Mary Roberts, comforted me on my numerous stays. She read to me and checked in on me during the long nights. After this, my most vivid memories of early childhood are of the preventorium.

My brother and I didn't attend my father's funeral, which was held in Monticello, Mississippi, at a small church. We played outside the church as a friend watched over us. Nor did we go to his actual burial in the small cemetery there. Years later, we visited the cemetery regularly with our mother so she could place flowers at our father's grave. Ned would get out of the car and go with her, but I never wanted to get out of the car. I always crouched down on my hands and knees on the floor behind the driver's seat, with my hands on either side of my eyes, shielding them from the sight of the graves around our car.

Ned and I did attend calling hours, held at the Tudor-styled Wright and Ferguson Funeral Home in downtown Jackson. The rooms were crowded with callers. My father, a charming man, had been popular in the church and city. I stood watching from across the room. My mother sat on a low couch surrounded by people. Each one would say something soothing to her, but her head never moved, nor did she look at anyone. She leaned forward, one elbow on her knee, holding a cigarette, from which smoke drifted up and the ash grew longer and longer. The air was filled with cigarette smoke.

I wandered through the crowd, noticing the colors of the dresses and suits of those present. Most wore dark clothes, black or navy or even brown. Ladies wore simple and severe hats with short veils, and most were wearing or holding gloves. If they were smoking, ladies took their gloves off.

There was a hat and coat stand in a corner of the entryway, loaded with men's hats and coats. I positioned myself under some of the coats hanging above me, trying to hide so I could look around the room. I thought about putting my hands in pockets but instead held onto the ends of the sleeves of two different suit coats, holding them as if they were hands, and swaying slightly side to side.

Across the room, I saw flower stands, elaborate with ribbons or some simple, that were thickly clustered together on either side of the casket. I let go of the coat sleeves and went over to my father's coffin. My head was exactly eye level with the edge of the coffin. I could see the satin, padded interior surrounding him. The strong fragrance of flower stands filled with lilies and carnations overwhelmed me. To this day, lilies and carnations are the scent of death and funerals for me. The sweet and peppery odor of carnations takes me immediately back to the open casket, scrutinizing my father, searching his face and folded hands for signs of life. His face was level with mine and if I moved just so, I could see a glimmer of his eyes underneath his lashes. I was sure he was alive and at any minute would open his eyes, see me, and smile. I reached out trying to touch him inside the casket. I turned to the group of men next to me and cried out, "I can see his eyes. He's alive. Come get him out."

For one shocked second, everyone near the casket was completely still and silent. All at once, people rushed toward me,

Susan, age four months, with father

pulling me away. A woman kneeled down next to me and said in
a soothing low voice, "Hush, honey, you don't want your mama to
hear." She looked intently into my eyes. "Your daddy would want
you to act like a grown-up girl."

"But," I faltered, "I can see his eyes. He's looking at me. He's not
dead. Look, you can see his eyes!"

"Honey," she said, "sweetie-pie, let's go find your mama and you
can give her a hug to help with her sadness." She took my hand,
gently leading me away from the casket. People were milling
about again, as though nothing had happened. As we made our
way through a sea of suits and dresses, I kept glancing back, still
convinced that I alone knew he was alive. This was my secret now.

Mother with Ned and Susan, 1956

I believed that he would come home again. For weeks and months after, I waited and waited, but he never returned.

As we drew closer to the yellow floral sofa where my mother sat, she looked up at me. She held out her arms, and I climbed onto her lap, where she hugged me close. I could see unshed tears in her eyes as she stared straight ahead. I leaned in and smelled her neck, touched her pearls, and then slid off her lap and onto the seat next to her, sitting as close as I could.

One of my mother's friends sat down next to me. She wore a navy-blue dress that featured a full skirt with a skinny, navy-blue belt at the waist, elbow-length sleeves, a turned-up collar, and big pearl earrings. She carried a pair of short white dress gloves and wore a navy hat that looked like something I'd seen a soldier wear. She cuddled close to me, smiling and leaning over to talk to me. There was bright red lipstick caked in the corners of her mouth.

"Susie, honey," she said, "how are you doing, sweetheart?" I gazed at her mouth with the heavy lipstick and didn't answer.

"You know," she said, "death is just like going from one room to another, closing the door and never opening it again."

Her words terrified and shocked me. The thought of being locked in a room forever, away from everyone, and never being able to get to my mother again horrified me. I jumped off the couch and ran to the door of the funeral home. I stood there, opening and closing it for the next fifteen minutes, until my grandmother came and pulled me away. From then on, I never allowed doors to be shut in our house except briefly. I constantly checked that any closed doors could open, and that I could go through them any time I desired.

8

Unknown Punishment

At the preventorium, I became two people: an obedient, smiling child on the surface and a watchful, self-reliant child within.

I persevered in trying to make sense of my world at the preventorium. I was self-reliant for emotional support, and I understood my existential aloneness, which gave me a kind of freedom. I had little social anxiety and never worried that I might not be the best or enough like the others. I was fine being different but had the added luck of knowing how to act like everyone else.

In photos, I look tiny, compliant, cheerful, and eager to please. I was all of these. I wanted to be liked by both the children and the adults, but I was fine if I was not. I was watchful. I learned to see their real selves, which they thought they kept secret. I saw nurses put forth their best selves for parents, the doctor, and each other, but in front of us, they behaved carelessly. They tended to relax and forget we were there. After all, children didn't count. They also assumed that we were not interested in them. I observed one nurse clean and file her nails, instead of watching the children running on the playground. When another nurse joined her, she quickly took the clipboard from under her arm and held it out in front of her as if she were perusing it.

Another nurse cast angry sideways looks at a fellow nurse, thinking no one would notice. Two nurses in a corner of a classroom were clearly gossiping about the teacher, whispering and grinning maliciously behind her, assessing her from hair to shoes.

I saw them.

Then there was the beautiful new night nurse who did not wear a traditional nurse's uniform. Instead, she wore a very beautiful and inappropriate pale pink frothy peignoir gown and robe that floated around her like a cloud. She was slender and blonde and looked like an angel with her smile. But I saw the fiercely hard pinch she gave one girl on the back of her neck as we marched into the ward single file with our arms akimbo.

When the girl complained, who do you think the other nurses believed? I saw it but said nothing. They wouldn't have believed me, either.

That nurse had a system. She selected one little girl to favor with smiles and compliments when she was in front of other adults and then to torture with secret pinches when she thought no one was watching. Little girls, not realizing what lay in store, looked up proudly at the beautiful nurse as they were selected to lead the group of girls into the ward at night. Later, silent tears of shame coursed down cheeks as not one of them wanted to be the one to complain and so bore the pain of the pinches.

As the beautiful nurse looked the group over, choosing her next victim, I moved behind taller girls. I was fascinated by her guile, her effortless charm, and how she could present herself one way but be an entirely different human being. These were discoveries that I kept secret. Someone must have seen her twisting the tender skin on the neck of a little girl, or the bruises left. She was there one day and gone the next. My mother later questioned if I really saw her wearing a pink nightgown and robe, but I was adamant. I remember because color of any kind was a rarity. And I remembered her charm, her ability to make people like her and want to be near her. It was a lesson I never forgot.

I and other former patients also vividly remember a nurse who seem to love paddling the children. She wore the usual white uniform and cap and had cold, dark eyes. We called her "the one stub monster" because her right index finger was missing the first joint. She carried a wooden paddle and tapped her shortened finger against the handle as she walked among the children. Most of us kept our eyes trained on that short finger tapping against the paddle, waiting to see who the next child who and hoping it would not be ourselves. During any of our structured daily routines, we learned to expect the sound of the wooden paddle popping against a thigh or upper arm. Not sleeping in the proper position? "Pop" went the paddle to turn the sleeper over onto his or her back. Not able to choke down the thick milk in one long gulping drink? A straw was given to the unlucky child to suck up the butterfat, and if there was even a tiny gagging sound, "pop" went the paddle.

For us, she was less of a person, less of a nurse. She was an enormous wooden paddle and a shortened finger tapping against the handle keeping a rhythm or, more likely, keeping count of her victims. Only once was I the unlucky recipient of the paddle. Early in my stay and unable to sleep, I had gotten out of bed one night. I wanted to walk around as I had back at home when I couldn't sleep. The one stub monster caught me in front of the nurse's station and popped the paddle against my thigh. The sharp pain shocked me. She put her finger to her lips to signal silence. Then she squeezed my upper arm hard and dragged me back to bed. I climbed in, stifling my sobs, tears squeezing out of the corners of my eyes. The next Sunday visit, my mother found a fading bruise. I begged her not to say anything. Who knew what would happen when she was not present, and who would believe children anyway?

All the children witnessed frequent spankings for those who forgot to keep both hands on their hips at all times while walking inside the building. If you let a hand slip a little lower than exactly at the midpoint of your waist while walking, a sharp and painful reminder was guaranteed.

One little boy was required to run and play, after he had sprained both ankles. It was extremely painful to place any weight on them, but during playtime outside, he was ordered to get up and run, so he did. Many former preventorium children recall the double standard on visiting Sundays held twice each month. For those days, we were often issued cotton, vee-necked shirts. Some wondered why we could not have them to cover our bodies the rest of the time.

Once in winter, we had a very rare snowstorm. We awoke to a view outside the windows that turned the world into a black and white vision, everything white except the dark bare trees against the white snow.

We ran to the windows to look at the dazzlingly bright, white snow covering the paths where we normally walked for exercise and the roof of the Brown House. On the playgrounds, the seesaws and swings were covered in snow. We longed to go outside but had no proper clothing to do so. We had to stay indoors the two days it took for the snow to melt. I wondered what my mother and brother were doing and if it had snowed in Jackson, too.

On the way to breakfast that morning, we excitedly broke our single-file line in the Circle Room to run to the windows and look outside. The nurse allowed us a brief viewing and then clapped her hands and called out, "Back in line please. Go on into the dining room for breakfast."

After breakfast, we filed into our classrooms, still excited about the snow. One little girl, fascinated by something so cold and soft and foreign, opened a window and had just started to reach out to touch the snow, when "pop," she received the blow of the paddle.

Some children were punished far more often than others. Was it because they did not have many visitors or none at all? Were they from homes where family could not visit? Were they forgotten or abandoned and therefore subject to the whims of the staff? With no advocates, they became targets for cruelty.

One former patient revealed to me that he witnessed sexual abuse by a staff person.

"There was at least one staff member whose interest in young boys was inappropriate by any standard. There was a degree of sexual abuse which I myself saw. That memory does not leave a person, although at the time I did not understand what was happening. The staff member I am thinking of disappeared suddenly and without explanation."

This was like the nurse with the pink peignoir.

While I was fortunate not to experience the worst abuses myself, I certainly saw my share of cruelty. It is shocking to see and experience the brutality of ordinary people. For some children, it was an unending nightmare. Others, including me, were emotionally frozen yet resilient and adaptable. While family visits mitigated some of the cruelty we witnessed, it did not erase the impact or memories.

Mealtime and food were another arena for punishment. Food often provoked extreme behaviors, both good and bad. The preventorium had a rule that if parents wanted to treat their child to ice cream, watermelon, or Coca-Cola, there had to be enough for all the children. We often had watermelon or ice cream on Sunday afternoons in the summer. About forty children in white bloomers sat on the ground, the swings, seesaws, or the concrete steps behind the building, holding thick, bright, pink-and-green slices of watermelon. When no adult was looking, boys took great pride in seeing how far they could spit the seeds. Some of them stashed little piles of seeds to use later, on the playground. Some girls joined in the seed-spitting contests as well. When the nurses noticed, they admonished the girls that this behavior was "not ladylike."

Coca-Cola came in the original small green bottles and was an enormous treat on weekends when families visited. It was brought out in wooden crates and set on a table. Parents and children lined up to receive a bottle to enjoy during their visit.

Ice cream was another special treat in the steamy, hot summers. Parents and friends arrived in their Sunday best, after morning church services, and everyone on the playgrounds, benches and in the fields, all enjoyed ice cream, in cones, scooped out of big buckets by a nurse or in little cups that came with a flat wooden spoon.

On birthdays, everyone gathered in the dining room to share cake. For my seventh birthday, my mother asked my aunt Mildred, her elder sister, to make a special cake for me. It was the fashion for little girls at the preventorium to have a cake with a doll in the center, surrounded by an enormous cake "dress." My cake had a curly-haired blonde doll, wearing a miniature floppy hat with tiny flowers, ribbon, and a lacy yellow top, stuck into a giant chocolate cake with yellow frosting, decorated with white flowers to look like a huge ball gown. Around the top half, white candles set into candy daisies in a circle.

The cake was so enormous that even after all the children, parents, and nurses were served, there was still a big cake remaining around the doll, although all the sections with frosting were gone. I was extremely excited and proud of this cake, but the doll, like the rest of the cake, went home with my mother.

Although our regular diet did not vary much, we enjoyed delicious fried chicken, buttermilk biscuits, and succulent pork chops with many southern vegetables, including fried okra, butterbeans, red, ripe tomatoes, collard and turnip greens, purple hulled peas with pink eyes that that my mother called "field peas," and yellow squash. Cornbread, a southern staple, was often served at supper, and cornbread leftovers were saved. Sometimes for supper, children were given hard cornbread soaked in buttermilk in tall glasses. This was considered a punishment for children who did not eat their meals at noon time. Ironically, almost all of us loved the cornbread and buttermilk supper. It was a source of secret fun that the staff thought of it as a punishment. Sunday night supper was often tomato soup, probably canned Campbell's soup, and grilled cheese sandwiches. But along with these delights, there was also food that I abhorred, like eggs, rice or tapioca pudding, egg custard, and especially the milk.

The full-fat milk served was unlike any milk I'd ever seen or tasted. It was thick and smelled strong. I could not determine what or why it had such a strong odor. The yellow color was not a warm yellow but a screaming yellow, like a Crayola crayon. Not many children liked this milk. Everyone who was at the preventorium has a story about the milk. Once, when talking with former patients, I mentioned that I had originally thought vitamins or something were added to the milk. Everyone laughed and reminded me that we were drinking "butter."

One of the few times I got into trouble at the preventorium was because I refused to drink the milk one day at breakfast.

Breakfast typically included eggs, which I loathed, plus some combination of fruit, toast, bacon, ham, and grits with butter, and always the dreaded yellow milk. We often had soft-boiled eggs in little egg cups and were taught how to properly crack the egg shell. I especially did not like these eggs as I thought they were raw. Other children loved them. The milk was served in glasses and sometimes in little bottles with the butter/milk fat on top. I was very obedient and wanted to please the nurses, especially at first, but after several months, I could not abide that milk anymore.

The nurses or attendants at each table engaged us in polite conversation. When it was my turn to contribute, I asked as politely as I could, "Don't y'all agree that this milk is not good at all? I really don't like it one bit." I smiled as I talked, thinking this made my statement stronger.

A number of the children at the table nodded. But the nurse sternly reprimanded us.

"You should be grateful to have this food prepared and available to you. You will not waste one bite of food nor one drop of milk," she emphatically stated. She must have remembered the rules about polite conversation because she suddenly smiled, which was as terrifying as if she were frowning and smiling at the same time.

"I would be happy to give my milk and eggs to anyone who would like them," I offered. "They will not go to waste that way."

I was proud of my well-thought-out suggestion and chose my words carefully, speaking slowly, as I thought that would make me seem more polite.

"I volunteer not to have my milk or eggs." I smiled broadly at everyone, struck by my brilliant idea.

One by one, the children at our table began to offer their milk to others as well.

"Maybe you would like it, Nurse?" I offered. She ignored me.

The nurse stood up, directed us to finish up, and drink our milk before we moved to our classrooms.

I decided I was done with this yellow milk.

"No, thank you," I said. "I will pass on the milk and am happy with what I've had."

The nurse's demeanor changed to extreme sternness. As the others were filing into a single line to go to class, she instructed me to stay seated.

"Susan Annah Currie, you will sit here until you have finished your milk."

"We'll see about that," I thought to myself, watching everyone leave the dining room, some of them shooting me quick, sympathetic glances. I calmly rearranged my silverware, the flowers in the small vase on the table, and pushed my plate with the cooling, dried-looking eggs, and the glass of yellow milk as far away from me as possible.

After about an hour, a cook came out, took my untouched glass and plate into the kitchen, and returned to take me by the hand to my classroom. I thought I had escaped ever having to drink that milk again, but I was wrong.

Over the time I was there, I choked down endless glasses of it. Once I attempted to soak up some of it with one of the big cloth napkins we had at every meal. I managed to soak up about half of the dreaded stuff but had to drink what was left, which was only a little liquid and the disgusting butterfat. Once I "accidentally" spilled it onto the table. I jumped up, apologizing, but the nurse immediately signaled for another glass to be brought to me. The cook and dining room attendant had to change the tablecloth, while the children all held up their plates and silverware. The attendant picked up the flowers while the cook shook out the new tablecloth, letting it float onto the table. Our table was a bit delayed in leaving the room because of this.

I still had to drink the milk.

Most everyone had a physical, visceral reaction to the milk, but the afternoon milk was the worst. Imagine being called from naptime, sleepy and just awake from a deep sleep, to drink down thick milk laden with butterfat or in the heat of playing on a summer's afternoon, having to stop to choke it down. We saw so many children punished for not wanting to drink it. One little girl was paddled almost every afternoon until her friends and some of the older girls started to take her glass and quickly drank the last of the milk butterfat with their straws while the nurse had her back turned.

Sometimes even now, when I wake late in the night and let my mind wander, it goes back to the formal, beautiful, and cruel dining room of the preventorium, where one of my worst memories of the preventorium occurred.

One little girl, who was tiny, beautiful, and sweet and who had curly blonde hair that sprang from her head like angel wings, could not get that awful milk down. The attendant at her table kept threatening her if she didn't finish it.

Before any of us knew what was happening, one of the nurses put her underneath the table in the center of the room to drink the milk from a baby bottle. I heard the laughter before I saw her. Her ankles crossed one over the other, and her head was bent down, the bottle at her mouth. She glanced up every so often, at the room full of children and adults laughing at her. She cried while everyone laughed and vainly tried to suck the butterfat from that bottle—it was impossible, and the nurse must have known this.

I put my hands over my ears to try to drown out the mocking laughter. I could not watch. Why, why would we laugh at this? Especially when any of us, at any moment might be humiliated, too? Whenever I think of that little girl and the tears squeezing out of the corners of her eyes, my chest tightens and my heart beats too fast. My hands begin to tremble and sweat, and I feel a hot flush coming up from my chest.

I have wondered about her so often. What memories was she left with? How did this experience shape her later life? Humiliation was the punishment of choice at the preventorium, although the paddle provided a swift and immediate response. No one thought about our psyches, our souls. So many children were taunted and humiliated, both physically and emotionally, by the adults.

That afternoon, on the playground, the little girl's older sister approached each child, shoving him or her in the chest with her hands and saying, "You laughed at my sister! I'm going to beat you up for that." Some children simply looked at their feet, refusing to meet her eyes. I protested, "I barely looked. I couldn't."

I began to cry as she pushed me twice, causing my feet to stumble.

"I didn't laugh!"

Then she went on to the next child. At least this little girl had a sister to defend her. Many others had no one.

Perhaps because her sister was there to support her, she recovered.

Another little girl had her hand beaten sharply with a comb because she wanted to comb her own hair. Like others, she was locked in a bathroom for hours until she had "done her business." Many of us, myself included, were made to sit at the dining table during meals until we had finished everything and were punished if we refused. One girl sneaked away, threw up, and then still had to go back to the table. She did not gain weight unless someone visited her. Weight gain was tracked constantly as a signal that a child's health was improving.

Another time, a little boy was brought out to the flagpole right after dinner at noon and given a small toy bowl of dirt and a spoon. He was made to eat as much of it as he could choke down until the "exercise" period was over. He had gagged on his bottle of tepid whole milk with its soft butter topping. He wrote to me years later that he took quiet pleasure in the fact the dirt was more palatable than the "direct-from-the-cow-teat unstrained milk."

A little boy had been jumping up and down in the Circle Room, pretending to be a monkey to make us all giggle. He was an adept performer. The nurse said that if he acted like a baby, she would make him a baby.

She grabbed him by the wrist and dragged him out of the room. When he returned, he was wearing a diaper. Some children laughed, while others hung their heads in shame for him. I felt a burning in my chest as I watched him slump in a chair, his eyes on the floor. For several weeks after, he hung back, unable to make eye contact. Over time, he seemed to return to his normal self, but I always wondered if he was marked psychologically. Does that memory come back to him now?

These scenes often return to me in the middle of the night. They are unbearable to remember.

At other preventoria across the country, even worse punishments were inflicted. Adults assumed that children would just "get over it" and be okay. There was also disparate treatment of children, often based on socioeconomic status. Children whose parents came every "Visiting Sunday," especially those who lived nearby, rarely bore the brunt of the harsh discipline. While the Mississippi Preventorium prided itself on the range of socioeconomic levels of its patients, from children of poor farmers to children of more affluent families, the children of those in higher socioeconomic levels received better treatment from the staff. Many of the girls at the preventorium speculated that boys were often treated more harshly.

Even though there were individual moments of kindness and tenderness, few children, myself included, viewed the staff as benevolent and kind. I tried to make myself invisible, understanding instinctively how to avoid being noticed. But I was a child, tiny for my age, and ripe for punishment like everyone else.

One morning I simply refused to drink the milk. I sat in my chair, frowning, and staring down at my lap with my arms crossed over my chest. The nurse at the table said nothing. At the end of the meal, she ordered us to replace our napkins in the rings as usual and to walk single file into the schoolrooms.

As we got ready to go, the nurse grabbed my hand, yanked me from the chair, and marched me into the classroom. She ordered me to go sit down and whispered something to the teacher. The teacher, who did not look particularly happy about the situation, called me and another little girl to the front of the classroom. I bounced up and proudly marched to the front. The other little girl, whose name I no longer remember, walked slowly, dragging her feet, her head hanging down. We both stood facing the class.

With the nurse watching, the teacher told us to repeat fifty times, "I will drink my milk."

Having seen so many other children in similar situations, I had mentally prepared for this moment. At night sometimes, I would rehearse what I would do if I got into trouble because of not drinking my milk. I gazed at the audience of children, ready to mock me and laugh at my punishment. I would not give them the satisfaction. I would not allow myself to feel that cold simmering heat of humiliation.

I smiled at the nurse and the teacher. I twirled from side to side, my hands out wide, my knees dipping one at a time as if curtseying and dramatically accented certain words, "I (arms wide), **will** drink my **MILK** (knees dipping and swaying side to side)."

The class, clearly delighted with my performance, began to join me in repeating the word "milk." The teacher said nothing. The nurse was just opening her mouth to stop me when the schoolroom door opened, and a staff person motioned me out of the room, saying, "Susan has unexpected visitors."

Behind her, I could see my paternal grandmother and step-grandfather. They peered through the open door over the shoulder of the staff person. They seemed curious about what was happening. I continued my performance. The other children seemed delighted by my defiance but also fearful of what would happen next.

The nurse was startled at seeing visitors, and extremely uncomfortable that I was being punished in front of them. I could see it in her sudden motion forward, her uncertain stance, and her eyes shifting side to side. Midmorning on a weekday was a very unusual time for visitors. My grandparents had driven from Corsicana, Texas, to Magee, Mississippi, and were planning to then drive north to Jackson to visit the rest of the family. The teacher clapped her hands and asked for quiet. The other little girl scampered away to her desk. I proudly walked out of the room to greet my grandparents. I did not look back at the classroom. I was delighted to have visitors on a school day. In any case, I knew that particular punishment was over.

My grandparents and I were taken to the big wraparound porch that connected to the two classrooms for our visit. This outdoor room had very pretty patio furniture with cushions that had a pattern of huge flowers.

My grandmother asked me, "What in the world was going on in class when we first arrived? Were you entertaining the other children, or were you in trouble?"

I told them about hating the milk and how I had refused to drink it and how I was made to stand in front of the class. I also told them I had refused to let the punishment upset me. Both my grandmother and grandfather teased me about getting in trouble, but my grandmother also said, "Quite right to stand up for yourself. After all, you are a Currie."

By this time, I was focused on the huge new baby doll my grandmother had in her arms. It was in a big cardboard box with a clear cellophane cutout in front so the doll could be admired. It was plastic, of course, with painted-on reddish curls, pretty, soft, white pajamas with ribbon around the neck and sleeves and tiny, white Mary-Jane shoes with little white socks trimmed in lace. The new plastic had a wonderful fragrance that I loved—the "new baby doll" scent. I held that doll for the entire visit, holding it close so I could inhale its newness. My grandparents took a photo of me with the doll to give to my mother.

We did not have a long visit, perhaps an hour and a half or so. My grandmother asked me questions about what we did during the day, what we ate, and where we played. I held the doll as a nurse gave us a tour of the girls' wing, the half-circle playroom at the end of the ward, and the playgrounds outside. My grandmother patted my head or squeezed an arm around me as we walked, clearly tickled at how much I loved her gift, but when it was time for them to go, the nurse gently took the doll from me and explained the rule about no special gifts. She asked them to take it to my mother to keep for me when I returned home. I was sad to give the doll up. When I returned home months later, it was waiting in the small white rocking chair in my bedroom.

◆ ◆ ◆

My grandmother, Aileen, was my father's mother. She had been widowed and remarried before I was born. When she visited us at our home in Jackson, she would tell my brother and me funny stories about our father and how mischievous he was as a boy. I liked to imagine him as a boy but pictured him looking just like he did when he was alive only smaller. I imagined him on a bicycle wearing his dress shirt, tie, and suit pants.

His father, my grandfather, McOyd Currie, was a doctor and Scottish to the bone, she told us. After he died, Aileen had married a widower. Charles, whose nickname was "Pete," was our step-grandfather. He was wonderful to us: generous, loving, and kind. They lived in Corsicana, Texas, which was a long drive from Jackson. The town's only claim to fame was that it was called

New baby doll

the "fruitcake capital of the South," thanks to the Collin Street Bakery, which is still in existence and selling its famed fruitcakes worldwide. I thought of Pete as a cowboy because he was from Texas, swore a lot, and had worked for the Texas Railroad. He was short, slight, and balding. He embraced his role as our grandfather, always giving us a quarter or two, and telling us stories about the railroad. My grandmother had gone back to school after her first husband's death and had become a licensed practical nurse. That was the only time my paternal grandparents came to visit me at the preventorium.

Easter bunny

I had very few other visitors. My mother always came for family visits, sometimes with a friend or relative but mostly alone. Once, our next-door neighbor, whose little girl and I had become friends briefly before I left for the preventorium, came to visit and brought greetings from the neighborhood.

My mother always brought along my father's camera and took photos of me in my little white cotton uniform. If she had gifts, she photographed me with them, particularly an Easter basket and bunny she brought. The basket held colored plastic and a fan. The Easter bunny wore flowered overalls and had a straw hat with holes for the bunny ears to protrude out of the top. I loved this gift and happily posed for a photo holding the bunny.

One time, Aunt Bessie, who had accompanied us when I first arrived at the preventorium, came with my mother. I was happy to see her bright red lipstick and listen to her constant stream of conversation. She always said whatever came into her head, who was wearing what, the state of the lawns, endless advice to my mother, all while gazing around and collecting information to take back and share.

My mother was constantly embarrassed by Aunt Bessie, but my brother and I loved going to her house where there were gorgeous antiques, like our great-grandmother's ornate vintage pump organ. It was placed next to a matching set of three-foot-tall lamps on end tables. The lamps were huge statues of a drum majorette and drum major, both holding batons in front of them, each with braided suit tops in white. The girl drum major wore a red box-pleat skirt, and the boy drum major wore red pants with a white stripe down the sides. Each wore white boots, with one foot raised up in front as if just starting to march, the girl's boot with a tassel in front. The electrical pole that held the lamp shade came out of the middle of their drum major hats.

Aunt Bessie always called me "Baby" and hugged me incessantly when she visited the preventorium. She always gave either the best or the most inappropriate birthday and holiday gifts. We never knew what to expect. Once, I received an old-fashioned beer can/soda pop opener, gilded, with giant fake rhinestone gems scattered over it and a round plastic disc in the middle. On the disc was a silhouette outline of the state of Mississippi. I was not yet fifteen. She thought I would like it because of the "jewels," as she called them. My mother was horrified at this gift, saying I was too young to have it, but Aunt Bessie winked at me behind my mother's back, saying that I could use it to open Coca-Cola bottles. I still have it. But her gifts might also be old potholders from the back of a drawer, elaborately wrapped up, or a pair of plastic Tupperware salt and pepper shakers she had on hand. We always looked forward to whatever surprise or disappointment her gifts might turn out to be.

The minister of our Presbyterian church also once came to visit me in the middle of the week. The nurse called me off the playground to see him. He was a kind, calm, and gentle man, but a forceful and intelligent preacher at church. He commanded attention, yet when we left church each Sunday, he always rested his large hand on top of my head, gently, reassuringly. I loved him even though I didn't always understand the sermons he preached.

When he visited me at the preventorium, he brought me a "LifeSavers Sweet Story Book," which held ten different rolls of candy. I was delighted and immediately looked for my favorites, trying to eat as many of the cherry candies as I could while he was there. I knew that after he left, the candy would be taken away.

What did the preventorium do with all the gifts, candies, and treats brought by visitors? Did the staff enjoy them in the evenings when we were asleep? I imagined my book of LifeSavers, minus the roll of cherry ones, being passed around to nurses at night, each one picking her favorite, unwrapping all of the candies at once, as I had done, and stuffing them into her mouth.

9

School Days

The preventorium boasted a certified public school for its patients. I began school upon my arrival at the preventorium, even though the school year was nearly over. I had just turned six, and I was assigned to the first-grade class, even though it was May and I had missed most of the academic year.

Everything was so new to me as we all lined up after my first breakfast, leaving our seats to form a single file. We marched out with our hands on our hips and went to the two school classrooms opposite the dining room.

Back home, I would have joined the first grade at Marshall Elementary School later that year, in September. At the preventorium, none of the classes were very large, and unlike traditional schools, the grades were merged. This meant the teachers had to adjust the teaching to cover several grades. In addition, the school day was only half a day, as the primary mission of the preventorium was building up the children's physical health. Education was secondary to that mission. They believed that restored health would enable children to easily catch up on any missed education.

The classroom was small. There were only three short rows of desks. At the very front of the room, the teacher's desk had books held with bookends on one side and, in warm weather, a small vase of flowers. Off to the right was a small table with four chairs, two small and two regular sizes. Behind the desk was a blackboard, and to the other side were low bookshelves full of books. A strip of bulletin board above the blackboard featured posters with letters and animals. At the back were low, round tables and child-sized chairs for crafts. An area with folding doors opened to display wall maps and another small bookshelf. Our windows overlooked the small lawn between the girls' ward and the classroom. At the back, there was a large, screened-in porch.

The teacher had short, curly, brown hair and wore a plaid dress with a matching belt and full skirt. She smiled at me as the children separated into their assigned classrooms. She asked my name and took my hand.

"Good morning children. This is our new classmate, Susan. Let's make her feel welcome."

Some of the children smiled, some looked out blankly over their desktops, and some giggled and talked, not paying much attention.

I did not feel especially welcomed, but I did not feel afraid. I gazed slowly around the room at each face, some bored, some staring out the window, some with their heads sunk down in a sad way. I found all of them interesting. What were they looking at outside the window? I could not see anything but treetops and sky from where I sat. I wanted to daydream, to begin imagining a whole other world, but I knew this was not the time. I refocused on the teacher, waiting to see what would happen next, still wondering about the children who seemed sad. Were they homesick? So far, on my second day, even with the strange and unfamiliar routine, this seemed to be an adventure. Even when I thought about my mother and brother, I did not feel any pangs of homesickness. I went to the desk the teacher pointed out to me and slid onto the wooden seat.

The desk had a dark slot at the top for pencils and opened to an empty space underneath. It was much too high for me. As I sat with my hands clasped together on top of the desk, they were almost parallel with my chin. There were fewer of us in the first- and second-grade classroom than in the other classroom, where

I could hear desktops falling with a bang, books being dropped onto desktops, and students laughing and moving around, their feet scuffling on the floor.

The teacher went to a shelf and pulled off a stack of books, which she distributed to each student. She read the first page and then asked the first student in the first desk of the first row to read two pages. The book on my desk was a *Dick and Jane* primer with vivid illustrations of two girls and a little boy. While listening to the readers, I leafed through the pages, finishing it well before it was my turn to read. The books were short, so when the end was reached, the next reader started over.

When it came time for me to read, the teacher came to stand next to me. I flipped the book back to the first page and read the entire story aloud from beginning to end. She said nothing but simply went on to the next child. At the end of the reading session, she passed around construction paper and small boxes of crayons, instructing us to draw a picture of an animal we would like to have as a pet. Then she came back to my desk, crouched down, and asked, "Susan, do you know how to read?"

"Yes, ma'am. My father taught me years ago," I said proudly. "We read the funnies together in the paper when we got home from Sunday School. We read *Dennis the Menace, Nancy, Brer Rabbit*, and others."

She went to the bookshelf and pulled out two books for me. I was deeply involved in drawing a picture of our black-and-white border collie, Tippy, with a bone in her mouth, which I had somehow made larger than her head, but I stopped when she brought the books and asked me to read them aloud to her. "Please read them again," she said, so I read them again from beginning to end. The next morning, when we entered the classroom, she called me over to the bookshelf and told me to pick out any three books that interested me. I spent as long as I could making my choices until she told me to go to my desk. I walked proudly to the desk, holding the books tightly to my chest and slid into the seat. When she began distributing the *Dick and Jane* books to everyone else, she said in a low voice as she passed my desk that I could go to an unoccupied chair in the back of the room and read by myself.

"Is it okay that I know how to read? Am I in trouble?" I asked and was relieved to see her smile.

"No, it's wonderful that you know how to read so well," she said. "We don't want to slow your progress down."

The school year was soon over, and I did not go to school again until late August 1959, when I was again assigned to first grade.

Again, because I could read so well, I was given permission to go directly to the back of the room to read. In fact, I spent most of my time reading, rather than participating in class activities. I was proud of this accomplishment and distinction, but in truth, it made things easier for the teacher. I was so engrossed with books and reading that she did not have to watch me as closely as she did other children. Ultimately, my preventorium school days were mostly filled with trips to and from the bookshelves, piling up stacks of books and happily settling down to lose myself in them. I read book after book each morning during reading lesson. This is one of the few fond memories I have of the preventorium. I can picture myself, a tiny, underweight girl, sitting in a chair at the back of the schoolroom poring over the books for hours. I reread every book in the classroom collection many times over.

◆ ◆ ◆

Among the letters and files my mother kept, I found my report card from the preventorium school. In the 1959–1960 school year, I earned high marks in "Growth in Skills and Knowledge" for reading and comprehension and reading aloud. I received A's in arithmetic, art, demonstrating reasoning ability, etc.

For "Growth in Habits and Attitudes," we got an "S" for Satisfactory, an "I" for Improving, or "U" for Unsatisfactory. I received satisfactory ratings for listening, following directions, playing well

MISSISSIPPI STATE PREVENTORIUM
SANATORIUM, MISSISSIPPI

ELEMENTARY SCHOOL

SESSION 19_59_ 19_60_

NAME _Susan Currie_ GRADE _1st_

TEACHER____

DEAR PARENT:

The purpose of this card is to show you how the Preventorium School is measuring the progress and development of your child. Our school is striving earnestly, as we work in cooperation with the health program of this institution, to give your child experiences which develop his physical, mental, social, spiritual, and emotional growth. We feel that thoughtful cooperation of parents and teachers is necessary for the development of happy, successful, democratic citizens. We welcome your help in meeting the needs of your child.

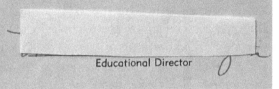

Educational Director

Report card

Classroom, courtesy of Elsa Clift Everling

with others, self-reliance, and politeness, but for the category of "Good Housekeeping," I had almost all "I's."

Good housekeeping was a category that I never understood. During one visit, I asked my mother what housekeeping could we possibly be doing? We weren't cleaning anything. I pictured our babysitter, Mary, washing dishes, or my mother making the bed. We did have to make our own beds every morning. I thought I did quite well as I pulled the sheets and coverlet up to the top of the bed and plopped the pillow on top. Everything was white, so it didn't seem to matter if I turned the edge of the sheet over the coverlet. Sometimes, in very hot weather, we slept on the bedding with no cover at all.

I had many "Unsatisfactory" ratings for "Uses Time Wisely." My mother told me on a Sunday visit as she reviewed my report card that I was too "chatty." That is what the teacher said. I didn't mind receiving an unsatisfactory rating. I did not often agree with what they considered "using time wisely." But I did not voice that opinion. I was adept at talking my way through situations, thinking rapidly to the next possible outcome calmly and strategically. Granted, my child's strategy was often flawed, but I knew that talking cheerfully, brightly, and smiling sincerely often protected me. And I was truly sincere in my cheerfulness. Even though at the preventorium, life was an extremely alienating experience, there was also so much that was fascinating. Little did I know I was gathering information for resiliency and strategic use throughout my life.

♦ ♦ ♦

We sometimes played games in school that were designed to teach specific lessons. We had a game to teach proper table settings and how to select a balanced meal from images of food and tableware. It was tempting to just make a meal of all the desserts, but I knew that would be unacceptable. There was also a game to teach safety when crossing the street, how to care for books with thoughtful handling, and several other educational games.

These games did not fool us. We knew that we were being trained to think a specific way about what is proper and correct. The games were supposed to teach proper meal decorum and style, but we found secret ways to be disruptive and amuse ourselves. Adults often missed little details like table settings being upside down on the mat, or a funny side dish like marshmallows being added to the dinner selections. Adults were so used to the routine, that they became bored and did not pay attention.

We children had a secret, nonverbal communication system that we used quite effectively, with facial expressions and eye and hand movements. When the adults were not paying attention, a great deal of quiet, subversive behavior took place. One little boy played air guitar every chance he got. It was a way of burning off excess energy for a child whose natural ebullience was curtailed. He played his "guitar" every time the teacher turned her back to write something on the blackboard.

♦ ♦ ♦

Through the window of the classroom, I could see the porch, the chairs with cushions in spring, summer, and fall, and what I at first thought was an enormous doll house. It was a square, white house, with a sloping roof, a wraparound porch lined with white columns, and floor-to-ceiling windows with green shutters. I learned later that it was a Louisiana-style raised cottage.

A nurse slapped my hand once as I reached out to touch it.

As a teenager, years after I left the preventorium and trying to forget the experience had ever happened, I had dreams about a "doll house" dimly remembered. In 1969, I read the newspaper article in the Jackson *Clarion-Ledger* about the little house that was on the screened porch. The article stated that it was "for the children's viewing and enjoyment," but it was really for show only. It had been a gift to the preventorium from someone VERY IMPORTANT, and it was, in fact, a replica of Beauvoir, the coastal home of Jefferson Davis. Memories of looking at this model house rushed back to me. I had not known the house on which it was based nor any of its history.

I remembered asking, "What good is it to have a doll house that none of us can ever touch?" But no one ever answered.

Visitors enjoyed strolling around it, exclaiming on its craftsmanship, and leaning down to look in the windows. I wasn't tall enough to see into the rooms through the windows. I wondered if the house had tiny furniture, like a four-poster canopy bed or a velvet-covered sofa with fringe. I vowed to one day see the rooms before I left, but never did. I thought I had imagined and dreamt so much about the preventorium, like this small model house, until, trying to prove to myself that the preventorium had ever existed, I found the newspaper article. Then everything clicked, and I had total recall of the model house. It is a strange and disorienting feeling to dream of something and later to have evidence that it was real.

We often wrote letters and postcards in school to our families. My mother bought a supply of postcards with kittens and puppies, clouds, and flowers so I could write to her each week. I carefully printed my "letter" to my mother each week, making sure to sign it "with love," as all the children were directed to do.

One time I was particularly eager to send my mother a postcard. This came after a Sunday visit. I had asked her how I came to be named, Susan Annah. She told me that I was named for my maternal grandmother; whose name was Anna. I loved that my middle name was spelled slightly differently, Annah. My mother's middle name, which she also loved, had come from a poem, "Evangeline." She wasn't sure where her first name, Nell, had originated. She also told me that my father was given a traditional Currie family name. There was always an "Edward" in the Currie family. She added that my brother had been named for my father. He was a "junior." I then asked why I wasn't named for her so we could continue the tradition of *her* name. I was outraged that I was not named Nell Evangeline Branton Currie Jr.

In class the next day, I decided to rename myself and mailed several kitten and puppy postcards to my mother signed, "Susan AND Nell Currie Jr." Eventually, I gave this up as I never received a response to my question about why daughters are not named after their mothers with a numeral or a "junior." I gradually forgot about adding "Nell" to my name and concentrated on trying to find one special thing to share in my cards and letters to her. I decided to do this after comparing notes with friends on the playground. I thought their notes and letters somewhat boring and predictable: "The weather is nice." "We played outside." "It rained all day yesterday." No, I wanted to be original! So, I tried to describe the flowers I found and how the moonlight looked through the windows at night. My descriptions were primitive and basic, but they were different from everyone else's: "The moonlight filled up the window"; "I made a pink and purple potholder in the Brown House"; "I lay down in a field of flowers and saw the bees looking down at me and the flowers"; and even, "I found a patch of stickers (thorns) outside in the weeds."

Some children said that the staff read every letter and postcard, and they cautioned me and the others to be careful about what we wrote.

"Never tell about punishments," one little boy warned me on the playground. "They keep those and don't send them. Then, they come and get you for punishment."

He continued, "I wrote to my mama and daddy about a paddling, and I know they never got it because I asked them if they had, and they said unh-uh, they didn't get it. I begged them not to say anything. And sure enough, I got a paddling after they left."

He looked around furtively at the nurses to see if they were watching him.

I listened with horror. I thought about this story every time I wrote to my mother and made sure to be extra careful.

♦ ♦ ♦

Hospitals are rarely quiet, although most have signs proclaiming the healing nature of quiet. The preventorium was deceptively noisy, even though there was no overt activity to make it so. For the majority of the time that I was at the preventorium, I experienced the hot bubble of heat and stillness of a southern summer. In the South, the late summertime hush is unlike any other. It is as if every bird, bug, and even the plants are holding themselves motionless to bear the humid heat.

The preventorium, set in the lushness of a green jungle of pine trees, blowsy, trailing flowers with fragrances so deep as to be almost sickening, was so quiet. It was as if a giant glass dome had been placed over the entire medical complex, trapping humidity, heat, and silence.

Winter there was drab and colorless outside unless the sun shone during the shorter days. The blue sky of winter was blazing in contrast to grey days and stood in stark relief through the mostly leafless tress, except the always-thick pine needles.

We were often commanded to "be still" when we came inside after playtime. Once, as we sat in the Circle Room just before supper at twilight, after a period of long silence, I realized there was sound in the thick tranquility: frogs, crickets, bees, and crows, and, occasionally, the wind blowing through the tall tree limbs. And there were all of us, the children, who maintained quiet unless given permission to speak. But even perfectly still and quiet, I could hear the sound of breathing, a sigh, the creak of furniture as we shifted positions.

There were many other subtle and obvious sounds: the quiet slapping sound of our bare feet on the dark, shiny, green linoleum floor as we walked single file, the odd sniffle, sneeze, or wheeze of a child in line, a stifled giggle or whisper, the sudden rush of breath being expelled when startled, and the hushed creak of doors opening and closing. I heard the teacher's voice in the classroom and the responding voices of the children, droning in unison. Chalk made a sharp tap as it first hit the blackboard and then a soft shushing sound. Desks opened and closed, and children occasionally gasped if a desktop was dropped down with a loud thud. There was the sound of the teacher's ruler occasionally rapping on a desk.

Pencils scrabbled across paper as we wrote postcards and letters to our families. I could almost feel the pencil tips dulling from the grinding of dozens of children bearing down on them. Dining was silverware clinking and glasses and plates being moved about the tables—an almost musical sound. Low conversation swelled into a soft rumble, sometimes growing louder and then falling into an unexpected, sudden lull. And there was the director's little bell, ringing, and the quick silence that ensued.

Released onto the playground, we erupted: running, laughing, talking, sometimes yelling, giggling, swinging rhythmically, flying high with a metallic clinking, the seesaw loudly creaking up and down, jump ropes on hard-packed earth sending up puffs of dust.

We could hear the far-off whoops of children on stick ponies riding among the tall grass and trees. And the sibilant sounds of children, holding stuffed animals or dolls, sitting together whispering. One little boy with a bow shot arrows with rubber stoppers into a target on a tree. The arrows made sucking sounds as they hit the target, and the boy yelped when he hit the bullseye.

And when afternoon milk was brought out, the glasses gently clinked together as the nurse lowered the tray. We fell silent. Then sounds of drinking, swallowing, and sometimes muffled gagging ensued, as some of us tried to hide our dislike of the milk.

We were quiet again as we marched back inside for "personal hygiene." As we waited in line, we whispered when nurses were not paying attention. The sound of running water grew louder as we moved closer in line to the bathroom. The two nurses wrote on clipboards to record our details, their pens scribbling on paper. During naptime, there were low murmurs as we chattered, going to our lockers, the metal doors clanging open and shut.

At night, complete quiet slowly descended as each girl settled into her bed. How can I describe the sound of little girls shifting on mattresses, settling finally on their backs, hands by their sides, trying to fall asleep?

At night if a nurse were not nearby, the chattering grew noisy. Some of the older girls invented a game. The hospital beds were lined against the walls of windows and had rails at the head and foot of each bed. A group of four or five girls would put their feet in between the rails, up against the wall, and then push themselves off as hard as they could. The goal was to propel the beds hard enough to bang into the lockers in the middle of the room and then to quickly launch themselves back from the lockers, all before the nurse caught them.

This activity made a thrillingly loud noise as feet slapped against the wall, wheels whooshed across the floor, and beds hit the lockers with a terrific loud crash. The lockers creaked back into place, and the beds thudded into place, with wheels hitting the walls. There was always one girl who didn't make it back in time, so this activity was often followed by the thwack of a paddle hitting her thigh and her sharp cry of pain dwindling to muffled whimpers. Slowly, slowly, the heat of the night air settled onto us all as we slept, and silence, punctuated by our breathing and sighing, fell over us.

10

The Most Girl Part of Me: A Brief Return Home

I smoothed the front of my dress with both hands. It had been a long while since I had worn a dress, but today, I had on a beautiful new one. It was a pale lavender dress and had a gathered skirt. I didn't even mind that my chopped pixie cut didn't go well with the dress. In fact, I didn't worry about my hair at all anymore, because every little girl at the preventorium had the exact same haircut, as did little boys. Fixing our hair was not a priority of the nurses. Except for our differing heights, all of us looked extremely alike in our small, white, sleeveless vee-necked cotton shirts, white bloomers, white sneakers, and socks. I often imagined that if all of us ran in the dark woods outside the building at night, we would look like small ghosts.

Standing there in my lavender dress with the puffed sleeves, I closed my eyes and pictured the ghostly white garments floating through the forest, the barest outline of children running through the forest, invisible except for the bloomers. Onlookers would become frightened while watching the fluffy white bloomers drifting through the trees, moving up and down seemingly of their own volition, floating clouds just above the ground.

Today, I was going home for a few days to have a tonsillectomy. I was not sure what that was, but on Sunday, during visiting hours, I had heard my mother talking with the nurses and the preventorium doctor. All I knew is that I would get to wear a freshly starched and ironed dress along with a new pair of shiny patent-leather shoes. I liked looking down at them as I walked across the dark, polished floor of the Circle Room to the reception room. I kept pacing back and forth, listening to the tap-tapping of my shoes and trying to get used to wearing them.

I had not been in the front reception area since the day I arrived at the preventorium.

Standing in the room now, waiting for my mother to come for me, I didn't know what day or even what month it was. We identified times of the year by season. It was spring outside when flowers sprouted, and the trees "leafed out," as my grandmother used to say.

I hadn't known I was going home until after breakfast when the nurse called me over. "Go back to the ward and change your clothes. Your mother is coming for you." I waited for more details, but none were forthcoming.

"Go on," she continued. "Go right to the ward, change, and then go to the Circle Room. I'll be along to take you to the living room."

I couldn't think of what I was to wear—I had only bloomers, but I obediently went to my locker. There, like magic, was the dress! I clapped my hands in delight when I saw the shiny patent-leather shoes. I thought of the shoes I had seen in the director's closet when Ethel and I sneaked up the stairs. These were as shiny and new as hers, and they were *mine*!

Oh, to be completely oneself just for a while and not one of a small army of little white uniforms marching in line. Because we had been deprived of individuality, we all faded into nothingness unless we misbehaved. There was safety in not being noticed, however, and I made sure to fade into the group while there were adults nearby.

I loved the new dress, with lavender bows at the waist and on the puffed sleeves. I could make it swish and swirl by turning side to side. Once I had changed, I hurried to the Circle Room, prancing a little to hear my shoes on the floor. Almost immediately, a nurse arrived and led me to the front living room, and then left. I was alone, but I could hear voices just around the corner.

On one wall was the table with the huge wall mirror I remembered from my first day. Since I was alone, with no adults anywhere in sight, I pulled a chair in front of the mirror and climbed on it so I could see my reflection. What a pretty dress! I jumped off the chair and began to pretend I was in a tap contest. I hadn't had tap dancing lessons, but I remembered one night watching tap dancers on the *Ed Sullivan Show*. I was captivated by their performance, how they kept their heads and upper bodies still as their feet moved faster than I had ever seen, and how their smiles never wavered. I remembered my father's funny tap dancing. I tapped and smiled, dipped and bowed to my "audience." Then I heard steps coming down the hall. I quickly moved the chair back and sat, demurely waiting.

I turned to see my mother. She was taking her car keys out of her black patent-leather purse, which made a satisfying snap when closed. She was talking to the director, who was behind her. They stopped at the director's desk, where my mother picked up some papers. Then they walked to the front doors. My mother held out her hand to me and I skipped over to take it.

"Susan, you be a good girl, now," said the director.

I said nothing but clung to my mother's hand. She smiled at the director, said thank you, and we went out the huge doors, past the enormous columns, down the stairs, and to our car parked in front.

My mother wore a belted, slim, navy-blue skirt and a white blouse with three-quarter-length sleeves. She had on a bracelet that I recognized from her jewelry box, where I used to spend hours going through her jewelry. One of my favorite things to do was to take out six matching "earbobs" as she called her clip-on earrings. I would invert the earring with the back clip flipped upwards. Magically, in my mind, the clip became the bodice of an elaborate ballgown and the inverted gemstone became the sparkling full skirt. I arranged the earrings in a circle and improvised dances for them on the dressing table. Sometimes I took my mother's perfume and lotion off the small gilt mirror tray and put the earrings on the mirrored bottom so that the sparkling gems reflected up while they swirled around as fancy dresses. To this day, when I see ballroom scenes of candlelight and dancing, I remember my mother's earrings on the mirrored tray and my staging of imaginary balls.

Now, holding her hand on our way to the car, I gazed at the bracelet and matching earrings. The stones were huge, heavy navy-blue, sapphire-cut crystals set in silver chasings with the underside setting cut in a flower pattern. I loved this set as a child and still have it. Many years later, I researched the stones and setting and learned the cut is called a "headlight" stone.

The bracelet clinked heavily on my mother's slim wrist, and the earrings caught the sunlight as we walked down the sidewalk to the car.

I slid onto to the front seat and moved over to sit as close to my mother as possible. She started the car and then took off the bracelet. She handed it to me asking, "Honey, do you mind holding this for me while I drive?" She knew I loved to look at the crystals up close. I played with it for quite a while, holding the stones close to my eye to see reflections in the facets, stretching it out on my leg and using it to measure the length from my knee to my thigh, putting it around my ankle to feel its heaviness and then, finally, just holding it in my hands.

As the car tires droned on the highway, I became aware of itching around my neck and the scratchiness of my dress. I was not used to wearing so much clothing and found it constrictive, especially the underwear!

We drove directly to St. Dominic's Hospital, where they admitted me and had me change into a hospital gown. I insisted that my pretty dress be hung in the tiny hospital closet so that I could see it, even if I was not comfortable wearing it.

Some of the nurses came by to greet my mother and remembered how often I had been a patient there. Sister Mary Roberts visited us as well.

"Well, you look tan and have more weight on you," she exclaimed.

She offered to stay with me while my mother went to get a cup of coffee, but my mother declined. They sat in the chairs at the end of the bed against the wall and chatted softly as I drifted off to sleep.

Later the doctor arrived and asked me to open my mouth and say "Ah." He poked and squeezed my neck gently.

"Well, Susan, would you like some ice cream?" he asked. "After we take out your tonsils, you can have all you want."

I liked that idea! I planned on eating only chocolate ice cream.

My surgery was early the next morning. I have few memories of it other than waking slowly, with a sore throat, and my mother sitting at the end of the bed with a magazine.

At some point, we left the hospital. I was very disoriented. It was strange to go to our house on Charleston Drive. My mother insisted I go to bed which I happily did as she brought me dish after dish of chocolate ice cream. She let our dog, Tippy, jump on the bed with me. Tippy continually licked my arm and face, and her tail thumped against the bed anytime anyone looked at her. Ned was more of a hazy memory as he must have been at school most of the time while I was home. I have a faint recollection of him standing in the bedroom doorway, grinning and talking.

During this four-day visit home, I must have interacted with people, but I have only vague memories of neighbors stopping by and my friend, Kathy, coming over to visit. What stands out is how I felt so odd, so out of place, like an alien. Even stranger and more disorienting was how everyone acted as if I had never been away. No one asked anything about the preventorium. I wondered about Ethel and the others. I knew every second of the day there, and what they were doing at the preventorium.

The only ones who knew about our existence were those of us who had been secreted away behind those columns and huge double front doors. This schism of two existences, one never quite intersecting with the other, was to follow me for many years. As I lay in bed at home, I remembered my father saying we can only exist in one place at a time, but I felt that a part of me also existed in Magee, Mississippi, in the hot sun, inside the preventorium, which was like a tiny time warp that was invisible except to its inhabitants.

11

Holiday

To the adults at the preventorium, we were little robot children, clones to be kept in line and controlled. We had no individuality in their eyes, except perhaps in the health records they meticulously kept for each of us. Perhaps when they looked at me, they did not see a blue-eyed, light-brown-haired little girl, but they saw "will not finish meals or milk" or "does not sleep through the night." There was a deep contrast between the severe routine played out every day and our inner lives and behavior when no adults were nearby. In secret corners, we whispered about what we liked or didn't like, what we missed, what we wished for, and what we dreamed about. The daily routine dehumanized us and protected us as it eventually dulled the attention span for all the adults watching over us.

Like an old film playing over and over, we repeated our endless routine in synch with each other, as instructed by the adults.

Holidays, especially Christmas, were the exception. The atmosphere of the entire institution loosened a bit, and even the staff seemed excited for the holiday. The rigidity lessened and children were not reprimanded for giggling and chatting while walking single file to and from meals or school.

A tall Christmas tree, decorated with ornaments and colorful paper chains we children made as part of our crafts activities, stood in the Circle Room. Greenery and holly branches with red berries were placed above the doorways, and poinsettias were displayed in the front reception area—the "Living Room."

The dining room, too, had tall holly branches and fragrant pine that was replaced throughout the season. In Mississippi, there are three kinds of holly with deep green leaves and bright red berries. Deep in the woods around the preventorium, holly grew so profusely that throughout the winter, beginning after Thanksgiving, the dining room always featured holly branches among the evergreen arrangements.

Christmas Day would be different from other days. We knew this not because anyone announced it but by the behavior of the nurses and other staff. We tried to eavesdrop on their plans for the day and night before the holiday. But it wasn't anything tangible that they did or said; there was definitely a feeling of festivity in the air. This was heightened by our arts and crafts projects. We made the colorful red and green construction-paper chains to decorate the tree and crafted holiday cards to give or send to our families. We were all delighted and surprised to walk through the Circle Room after supper one December afternoon to see a huge evergreen tree, reaching almost to the ceiling, positioned in front of the windows. That evening we all worked to drape onto the tree the seemingly endless loops of paper chains that we had made. The nurses helped us so that the chains didn't end up only around the bottom half of the tree. The next day, the tree was even more exciting as someone had woven lights throughout its branches and placed a gold star on top. We were thrilled by being able to walk by the tree as we went to and from classes and meals.

On Christmas Eve, we sat in a circle around the decorated tree and sang Christmas carols, hymns, and songs. Everyone, even the sternest of nurses, smiled and joined in. The director, too, was leading us in song. We all went to bed that night excited, giggling, and eager for Christmas day, when our families would visit in the afternoon, bringing us presents.

This was one of the few times during the year, perhaps the only time that nurses overlooked giggling and whispering. No one was disciplined, not even the four little girls who gathered in a circle, holding hands, and jumped up and down while in line for toothbrushing. That evening, little girls giggled and chatted throughout the ward.

The energy was still high, even when everyone was in bed. The nurses announced that we had to turn the lights out so that Santa could visit. Santa, we were told, would come to our preventorium in the middle of the night and leave each of us a filled Christmas stocking on our beds. This announcement energized some little girls even more; they were so excited at the prospect of Santa's visit.

I had long ago forsaken any belief in Santa Claus. Since my father's death, I had become distrusting and even cynical. That night, I lay awake for hours, alert for any activity in the ward, gazing out the window at the foot of my bed. At first there was a low, soft sibilance of whispering that was soothing as the night deepened and finally, there was silence. But I lay still, fully awake. I heard the nurse making her rounds of the ward, checking on sleeping positions and making sure that we were all asleep. When she got to my bed, she came to the side of the bed and bent down close to me.

"Can't you sleep?" she asked.

No nurse had ever stopped to talk to me in the long night. I lay silent.

"You need to go to sleep so Santa can come. He will only come to leave stockings for everyone if all the children are asleep," she told me.

She kept glancing over her shoulder to the ward entrance as she talked, and I wondered what was capturing her attention. Finally, she moved away from my bed toward the entrance where she held her hand as if she were stopping someone. I raised my head slightly and saw another nurse just outside in the hall.

I stayed motionless and listened to them whispering. After a while, I lifted my head again. The two nurses were hanging red net stockings on each bed in the ward. I lay still until one of the nurses had reached my bed. I stared up at her, wondering how my face appeared to her upside down.

She carried a red net stocking trimmed with red and white striped piping and tied with a red ribbon at the top. It was filled with peppermint candies and small toys. She held it out tentatively toward my bed, tilting her head as she stared at me. She seemed unsure what to do.

"It's okay," I whispered. "I don't believe in Santa Claus anyway."

Perhaps she was startled by my pronouncement, as she stood there thinking for a few seconds. Then, she put her finger to her lips to emphatically shush me and hung the stocking on my bed. She continued her rounds.

I waited until both nurses had finished and I saw them carrying the empty boxes out of the ward.

Then I carefully stood up on my bed, and gently unhooked the stocking to examine the contents. There was a small Santa toy, a snowman eraser, pencils, peppermints, and other small things. I put everything back into the stocking, retied the ribbon, rehung it quietly, and lay back down on the bed, making sure the sheets and blanket were straight. I thought about Christmas at home and wondered what my brother and mother were doing, if they were asleep or eating cookies together or decorating the tree. This did not feel like a holiday to me except for the laxness in enforcing the rules.

When the bell rang the next morning to wake us, everyone leapt up in their beds, excitedly whooping at finding the stockings. I took the stocking off my bed, loosened the top, and poured the small toys and candies onto the bed. When we went to our lockers for toothbrushes and other necessities, I stored as many peppermint candies as I could on the top shelf of my locker, pushing them to the very back so that I would have them for more than just this one day. I planned to have one each night as I tried to fall asleep.

Even though I did not believe in Santa, it was hard not to be excited by everyone else's happy anticipation. As we marched to the dining room in single file, we could see presents underneath the tree. We ducked down low, close to the tree, as we passed by the gifts, trying to read labels or size up the shapes of the boxes to guess what they might hold. Many of us were giggling and laughing, but there were also children who were somber and silent. Perhaps their families were not able to visit, even on a holiday.

In the dining room, the tall holiday arrangement in the middle of the room featured red ribbons and gold decorations. The director wished everyone a merry Christmas before saying grace for the meal. The kitchen staff emerged from the kitchen to stand with us. The director bowed her head and said a blessing for the holiday. Some of the adults said, "Amen."

When the director rang her little bell, we all took our napkins out of the rings at the tops of our plates, placed them on our laps and waited for the adult at our table to begin eating. Even on holidays, this routine was followed.

After breakfast, we filed into the Circle Room to join our families. I hugged my mother but watched the others. I held myself in check. I did not hug her with abandon or even behave gleefully as others around me were doing. I knew my mother would leave. And where was my brother? He was not with us. Was he with a relative? My mother and I smiled bravely at each other. She had brought me a gift—only one, as allowed by the rules. Originally, children were allowed to keep their Christmas toys for a week, but in my time, we could play with the gift this one day only. Then they went home with the families to prevent envy, arguing, and unfair advantage of some children over others with less.

For me, the highlight of the day was when girls and boys were, for once, permitted to visit each other's wards. I ran as fast as I could down the hallway to see the boys' ward. How disappointed I was to see the same double row of lockers down the middle of the room, white beds along the walls under windows, all surfaces scoured clean exactly like the girls' ward. I had hoped for something different, some clue that boys instead of girls lived in this ward.

After sitting around the enormous Christmas tree in the Circle Room, singing Christmas carols, opening our gifts, laughing, and visiting with parents, and running in the building as we liked, suddenly the routine was all too familiar. I had to say goodbye to my mother, who had been forced to spend one Christmas with me and a separate one with my brother. I wondered if he had thought of me at all. I missed him.

12

Found Memories:
Photos and Newspaper Articles

Among the photos taken at the preventorium, I found only one
of my mother, visiting on a Sunday afternoon. It is an old, 1959,
square, black-and-white photo. Taken at a slight angle, it shows
her sitting on a bench, her arms at her waist, her legs crossed.
She is wearing a checked sleeveless summer dress with a wide
vee neck and a full skirt, gathered at the waist, that spills onto the
bench. Next to her is a black leather handbag edged in metal, open
accordion style, the thin metal handle dangling on the right side.

She has an expression of unbearable sadness; her eyes have dark
circles underneath. She is beautiful in a tragic way with her wavy
short hair, her beautiful arms and hands. I can see the wedding
ring on her left hand in the photo. She never stopped wearing it
after my father's death. There is a photo of me searching in her
purse with a kaleidoscope nearby on the bench. I look happy to
have her visiting.

What painful burdens she had to bear: one child ill and in
the preventorium, the other, my brother, at a rambunctious age,
perplexed and sad at the loss of his father.

My brother and I lost contact during those fifteen months. We
had to adjust to each other when I was home for the tonsillectomy
and, then of course, when I came home permanently. For almost

Mother on Sunday visit

a year and a half, he had been the object of my mother's complete
attention, so having another child in the house must have been
disconcerting. We also had to get to know each other all over again.
It was difficult and sometimes awkward for everyone.

   When he did come to the preventorium, my brother was never
allowed to be near me. No visiting children were allowed to be any
closer than fifty feet. Somewhere, there is a photo of my brother
that I took at the preventorium, at a great distance from me. He
was playing alone on the front lawns and had approached the
imaginary border that he was not allowed to cross. He wore blue
jeans with the hems rolled up and a sleeveless, red and blue tee

Susan searching in purse

shirt. In the photo, he appears tiny, far off, his arms on top of his head, squatting so his knees are bent, and he is making a funny face at me. My mother always brought the camera and allowed me to take a photo or two. My brother and I vividly remember the day I took his photo and the shirt he was wearing.

I still have the camera that I used to take that photo. It belonged to my father and mother who took many photos of happier early years of our family. The camera is an Ansco B2 Speedex Junior, manufactured in Binghamton, New York, and it produced either two- or three-inch, square photos, depending on the film used. In those days, it often took several months to shoot enough photos to develop a roll. Some—but not all—are dated on the scalloped, old-fashioned edges of the pictures.

The first photos are dated June 1959, the first month my mother was allowed to visit after my arrival in May. The last ones are dated August 1960. They are not when the photos were actually taken but when they were developed. They were all snapped outside on the playground behind the girls' ward. Most are staged, and all children were prompted to smile for the camera. There I am, holding a lady's fan, dolls, or some other gift. There is one of me holding a toy rifle almost as tall as me. There are photos from Easter, one with an Easter bunny. There are cheerful photos of me with other little girls: in some we display toys or balloons, while in others we posed and smiled for the camera, as instructed. I can tell which photos were taken near the end of my fifteen-month stay, as I look confident. I had become completely adjusted to life at the preventorium. It was now the only life I knew.

A photo of Ethel and me is among my favorites. She stands behind me. Her eyes are dark, her arms wrapped around me and there is a slight smile of contentment on her face as she rests her chin on the top of my head. I'm in front of her, smiling, holding a Black baby doll, a gift sent to me by Mary, our daily caregiver at home, back when my father was alive and both parents worked. Mary spent every Monday through Friday with my brother and me. She was not allowed to see me while I was in the preventorium because she was Black.

My mother brought me the doll one weekend and told me it was from Mary so that I would not forget her. I did not know at the time that Mary was dying from cancer. With almost no exceptions, children were not allowed to keep the toys brought on Sunday visits. We mostly played with toys kept on site in the semicircle rooms at the end of the sleeping wards. But my mother insisted that I be allowed to keep the doll Mary gave me. I carried the doll with me everywhere during playtimes and allowed only Ethel to play with it. Once I entered the preventorium, I never again saw Mary. By the time I was released from the preventorium, Mary had died.

Mary had taken care of us when we were very little. One of my earliest memories is when I was one or two years old, and Mary was pushing me down the street in my stroller and holding Ned's hand. Our parents were at work. Mary lived near Jackson State University and walked to our house on Prentiss Street every morning. In the afternoons, when we drove her back to her house, all her grandchildren would run out to greet her, crowding around her and hugging her. Years later, I thought of how she had taken care of my brother and me, when she had so many little grandchildren who would have surely loved to have her home taking care of them. She cared for us as if we were her own children, especially after our father died. She cooked endless meals for us, told us Bible stories, and sat with us late in the afternoons.

In the spring and summer afternoons, Mary, Ned, and I would sit on the front screened porch of the little house on Prentiss Street, waiting for our parents. I was usually in a stroller or on the rocking horse with the yarn mane, while Ned played with toys on the porch floor. Mary was a powerful storyteller and orator. My brother remembers vividly a strong thunderstorm whipping through the branches of the trees over the porch, the lightning bolts and jolting shock of loud thunder shaking the entire house. He tremblingly climbed onto Mary's lap and ask what the loud noise was. Mary declared, "It's the wrath of the Lord."

Whenever I heard her say something like this, I pictured the small church on a corner near our house. In the front of the church was a life-size statue of Jesus with his hand on an enormous globe that lit up at night. I was fascinated with the globe and loved when we drove by it during the evening.

I was always grateful for Mary's presence, and as I grew older, I realized the bond she and my mother shared as widows, even though in those days, there was a rigid boundary between races. I was grateful for the help she gave my mother and how gentle she was, how she watched over my brother and me. She was funny, too, in trying to get us to eat healthfully. Once she had tried to fool us into thinking that the calves' liver she served us was a steak.

Upon my return home, I found a new babysitter, Gladys, who was very tall and also gentle. She called me "Baby" and gave me special attention. She told me folk tales and could make up elaborate stories on the spot. I had no photos of Mary to remember her by, but for many years I did have the doll she had sent me.

◆ ◆ ◆

In addition to personal photos, I have seen photographs from newspaper articles shared on social media or sent to me by my mother or by relatives and friends. The newspaper articles show smiling children playing games. I am in a photo taken for the Sunday edition of the *Clarion-Ledger/Jackson Daily News*, dated January 24, 1960. I would have been at the preventorium seven months by then. I don't have the accompanying article—just the newspaper photo of forty children, the director, and a nurse. I still look so small in that photo, although I must have gained weight and become healthier by then. The caption under the photo emphasizes that "no children suffering from tuberculosis, or any other contagious disease, are admitted."

I encountered another positive newspaper article, in a combined Sunday edition of the *Clarion-Ledger/Jackson Daily News* in February 1968, when I was fifteen years old and deep in denial. I do not remember reading this article that extolled the enthusiasm that the "alumni" of the preventorium had for their time there. It describes the routine, the schedule, and included stories of children thriving. It also mentions "life embellishment" from civic clubs and parents: records and record players. Perhaps later, some progressive activity had been added. It was not present when I was there, or at least I never saw any evidence of it. The leaders of the Mississippi Preventorium were always lauded for their work.

I find these Mississippi newspaper articles and photos fascinating. We children are clearly posing, smiling obediently for the
camera. The photos and articles applaud the benefits to children at
the preventorium. For example, an article from the *Clarion-Ledger/
Jackson Daily News* from June 1986, includes statements of grat-
itude from some former patients who felt the preventorium had
saved their lives. It surely improved my own physical health.
I weighed twenty-nine pounds as a six-year-old when I entered
in May 1959; I was the size of an average four-year-old. But I did
not remember the place as fondly as some seemed to do in these
articles. As I connected with former patients, I found that many
were emotionally scarred, even if their physical health improved.

The 1986 article lists "proper rest, a balanced diet, a regular routine, and fresh air and sunshine." The article quotes the director as
saying, "I've always said you can't get to first base unless you have
discipline.... The way we punished them was to isolate them. We
put them in a corner."

Did the director never see some of the horrible things that we
children witnessed and experienced? Perhaps she never knew of
the humiliating punishments and the paddlings? She was busy
as the institution administrator, and perhaps staff and nurses all
were as careful when she was around as they were when families
were present. The 1986 article describes the sleeping position we
all had to assume. It explained that if a child rolled over during
the night, the nurses would turn her onto her back, and that was
the case sometimes. But many of us were awakened in the night
by a paddle—not a gentle correction. Many of us did not trust the
staff because we had witnessed or experienced abuse.

There were children, of course, who were settled and happy as
if they really were at camp. One former patient was even quoted as
saying, "It was like being at camp all year." Some children loved their
stay and even kept in touch with some of the preventorium staff.

I couldn't even allow myself to think about the experience until
I was a teenager, and even then, I questioned my memories. I had

buried those images so deeply, I sometimes wondered if I had imagined it. Some of the punishments I witnessed came back to me unwanted when I least expected them. I could not bear to read or pronounce the word "humiliation." I hate the word still. It brings up images I have sought to bury but cannot. I accommodated to the routine, and I did not experience the physical punishments and humiliations some of the children suffered, but mine was not a happy stay. And I saw many, many children suffer emotionally and leave traumatized.

13

What I Never Told Anyone

Here is the part I never told anyone. After my father's death, I decided that I couldn't grow up anymore. Of this I was certain. If I continued to grow up and get older, my mother would die like my father—unexpectedly, suddenly—and disappear into the night. But how was I to achieve this? My four-year-old self could only think of one thing—to stop eating. Surely that would slow down the growing process so I would remain a tiny girl, and my mother would be allowed to live. I would not tell anyone so no one could stop me.

So I did. I stopped eating.

I was already sickly with asthma, but now I was severely underweight and became sick more frequently. I spent most of my fifth year of life at St. Dominic's Hospital. Upon turning six, I looked like a four-year-old and weighed just twenty-nine pounds. My plan backfired, though. I did lose my mother. She did not die, but I was sent away to the preventorium, in exile from her, my brother, and everything familiar and loved.

The preventorium was a badge of shame. No matter how much the medical establishment touted their cures, no matter how much the newspapers published articles, no matter how often visitors offered their false smiles and fake cheeriness, I knew I was branded now. I could see what they were thinking in everyone's

eyes: "Thank God it's not my child" or "Poor Nell, first she lost Ed, and now Susan has been sent away to the preventorium."

In addition, the fact that so many poor children throughout the nation were sent to preventoria added the taint of association with a disparaged group; being poor was considered shameful, particularly for poor, rural southerners.

During one of her Sunday visits to the preventorium, I finally told my mother why I did not eat. "I can't eat and grow," I burst out after she had been telling me that I needed to clean my plate at meals. "I can't. If I do, I will grow, and you will die just like Daddy did."

She put her face in her hands and began to weep. I was horrified that I had let my secret slip out and hurt her. I sat on the bench and squeezed myself as close to her as I could until she stopped weeping.

Before I went to the preventorium, she had tried everything, driving all over to find whatever I fancied. Once she drove across town to the one Chinese restaurant in town to beg them to sell her a bag of fortune cookies because that was all I wanted to eat. The owners of the restaurant thought she was a lunatic, begging for those fortune cookies. "But it's all my little girl will eat." They eventually relented and even gave her an extra bag. She thought I liked the sugary treat, but I actually liked to crack the cookies open because I thought I would find a fortune telling me that I wouldn't grow older and that my mother would be spared. Or that my father would come back, walk in the door, scoop me up in his arms as he did every afternoon, and ask me how my day had been.

I never found that fortune.

Instead, I was exiled at the preventorium and became a stranger in my own family, while they—my brother and my mother—went about their daily lives, establishing a routine that did not include me. They thought of me as if in the past. I was in a holding place, unchanged.

They could not understand the endless routine, the dehumanization, the loss of individuality. They assumed I was safe and cared for. They did not know I was being imprinted as a perpetual outsider and would never again quite fit in. I had been at the preventorium much longer than many children. It had taken me a long time to become so routinized, and once I was home, it was a foreign land to me. When I got home, I had difficulty forming close relationships. I had difficulty tracking days and times. I watched my mother and brother go about their daily routine, so different from what I had experienced. They seemed to have a separate language and a mutual understanding, I felt I did not belong with them. They expected me to pick up where I left off as if none of us had experienced any changes in the fifteen months I had been gone. We never spoke about my being away.

I was in my twenties before I ever told anyone outside my immediate family that I had been a patient at the preventorium.

Years later, I thought that perhaps we never broached the subject of the preventorium because each of us worried we might upset the other. Perhaps we were trying to protect each other by burying the bad memories. But I never forgot them. And I thought and dreamed endlessly about the preventorium.

◆ ◆ ◆

When I went looking for others who had been patients at the preventorium and found them on social media, we shared photos, experiences, and memories. This was a revelatory experience for me and confirmation that I had not imagined this strange past.

Their photos posted online drew me back into the aloneness of being in a crowd of children vying for attention in the rare times we were allowed to act freely and express our natural energy: the first burst onto the playgrounds and family on two Sundays per month and on holidays.

I searched for information over the years. With the internet, I found more than I had been able to locate easily via traditional resources. In addition to the information from other patients on social media, there is a silent video, digitized from a home movie someone's relatives made, of a visit to see one of the children at the Mississippi Preventorium. It appears to be Christmastime. The video opens with three well-dressed people, two ladies in 1959-style coats, complete with hats and gloves, and a gentleman in a light-colored suit with a skinny tie, walking up a tree- and shrub-lined walkway. One woman carried a tray with something covered on it—a cake? The video was in color, which brought the preventorium alive for me again, as all my photos are black and white.

In the video, one of the women steps in front of a table with candelabras decorated for the holidays. She moves quickly away as someone is asking her to move. The adults looked around the foyer. The next scene takes place in the classroom. In a flash, the video brought back memories of the classes. It also clearly demonstrates one of the few free, disruptive times at the preventorium. In the video, the teacher wore a plaid shirtwaist dress with a very full skirt, tightly belted waist, and three-quarter-length sleeves. The camera pans across the room where children make faces at the camera, wave, and smile. I recognized one little boy who was always hiding from the camera, covering his face with arms that were as thin as sticks. In typical fashion, he ran away from the camera to hide behind other children. And there was the other little boy I remember, whose pent-up energy was allowed to escape at last, playing air guitar furiously, moving his entire body. At one point, the energy of the children in the room, allowed to relax from the rigid routine, suddenly crossed over to that frightening edge for adults where children seem uncontrollable. Silently, the teacher moved back into view, her back to the camera, and rapped her knuckles on the desk. The children are immediately still, listening intently to what she is saying. As it was winter, all the children wore the sleeveless, vee-necked shirts in addition to the white bloomers.

In the video, it was as clear to me as it was when I was there which children were traumatized and which were more adjusted to the place. I could tell the shy ones from the bold ones. I recognized many of the faces.

Then the children are shown marching in single file, hands on waists. One by one, each child moved in front of the camera. The little boy who didn't want his photo taken holds his arm up in front of his face. And the little boy with too much energy was still playing air guitar. Child after child passes in front of the camera, a tall one, a tiny one, highlighting the rigidity of routine and the lack of individuality. All the little girls sported Cleopatra bobs with sheared-off bangs, and the boys had buzz cuts. On the faces of each child passing in front of the camera, I saw panic, fear, shame, boldness, and resignation.

To my surprise, I am the very last little girl, marching in line behind a much taller girl. I look directly at the camera and smile. I carry what looks like a gift box. Why I was the only one allowed to carry a gift I do not know. Seeing my tiny self, so much younger at the preventorium, proudly carrying a box, shocked me.

Following the children, the adults walk by in groups, or individually, smiling, and chatting. Many are carrying gifts; it must have been Christmas. A young woman in a red, high-necked dress with a tightly fitted bodice and raglan three-quarter-length sleeves, holding her handbag on her wrist, strolled past. She glances at the camera briefly, unsmiling. This is my mother, visiting for the holiday festivities before returning to her other life in Jackson and back to my brother.

The video is dated as being in 1962, but I was there from May 1959 through August 1960. The mislabeled video is additional confirmation of the lost history of this place. Even the name of the video erases its true nature. It is labelled "TB/Asthma Sanatorium." It is clearly the preventorium.

The preventorium loomed large in the lives of the patients, but the history of it is mostly forgotten or subsumed into the history of the Mississippi State Tuberculosis Hospital. If one looks at a map of that area of the state, Sanatorium is clearly labeled. Sanitorium,

Mississippi, was established as an unincorporated community with its own post office and train depot. It is a community in Simpson County, Mississippi, northwest of Magee, named for the Mississippi Tuberculosis Sanatorium. There is no mention of the preventorium.

◆ ◆ ◆

Many years later—when I was in my forties and visiting my mother in Jackson, Mississippi—I had a sudden desire to see the preventorium. For so long, since returning home at age seven, I had tried hard to put it out of my mind as if it had not happened. But now, I felt compelled to see it, to gaze at the entrance to prove to myself that I had been there and that it existed. I was aware that my mother had photos in a box underneath her bed, but I hadn't taken them out since my return home from the preventorium.

As my mother and I lingered over coffee, I asked casually, not quite making eye contact, "How far is Magee? How about taking a ride there this afternoon just to look at the old preventorium?"

"Okay," she said. "It's only about an hour from here. Why do you want to go?" She did not look at me either.

"I'm just curious," I responded.

She said nothing as we finished up in the kitchen. Then she picked up her purse and keys and we headed to the car. As we drove south, we chatted about her garden and what we wanted for supper that night but not about the preventorium. She may have been waiting for me to bring it up. I was in a heightened state of nerves and sat silently, chewing my cuticles and staring out the window. I watched the scenery flashing by and thought how little had changed along the highway. It was still countryside with few houses, thick forests, and, occasionally, gentle green fields. Every once in a while, we passed a farm stand, with offerings of peaches and tomatoes.

I was worried about this sudden desire to visit the preventorium. In some ways, I wanted to preserve it as it was in my memories of brilliant sun and whiteness in the hot summer. I wanted to remember only how I had created my own world in the midst of isolation and extreme routine. But it was the routine that allowed this form of self-soothing which had, perhaps, protected me from deeper trauma.

As she drove, my mother began to talk a little about the hours she spent on this highway and how difficult it had been for her and my brother. She didn't ask how it was for me during my time at the preventorium.

With a shock, I realized her experience of the preventorium, of course, was completely different.

Her memories of me were those of a child well cared for at a reputable institution. Because I had appeared cheerful and happy each time she saw me, she thought that I had been okay—even happy. Many of the photos show me smiling and looking happily settled. I pictured her arriving for visiting Sundays, seeing me smiling up at her, and happily receiving whatever gift she had brought. I must have looked composed and secure. Certainly, I was improving physically. And all of us smiled for photographs. Still, on this trip down Highway 49, I would have liked to express the alienation and loneliness that I felt then and when I returned home. Perhaps she could not bear to think that I was anything but happy since she felt she had no choice but to send me there.

I listened halfheartedly to her chatter, my thoughts elsewhere. My goal was to see the preventorium, to prove to myself that it existed, that I had actually been there, and that it was not a dream. After a while our conversation died out and we continued silently. I felt a heightened anxiety and barely remember most of the latter part of the drive.

It was a sunny spring day, I think. In all my memories of the preventorium, it is always bright, perhaps due to the light that reflected off all the white and shiny surfaces in the hospital.

Once we arrived in Magee and drove across the railroad tracks and onto the campus, my mother headed right to the curved driveway and stopped in front of the sidewalk that I remembered so well. Memory is a muscle. When it is used often enough, it creates automatic reactions. My mother never hesitated once in driving around what was a confusing campus. She had, of course, driven here every other Sunday for fifteen months.

We got out of the car. As we walked up that long sidewalk and past the enormous columns, now dingy, all I remembered is how I cheerfully offered to stay a week, not realizing I would stay for fifteen months.

The beautiful pendant light suspended from a long, heavy chain was no longer there. We pushed open the front door and awkwardly stepped inside. The staff stopped and stared at our sudden appearance. A woman came over to greet us. I briefly explained that I had been a patient at the preventorium as a child and asked if we might look around. She explained that the place had been turned into a daycare for adults with severe disabilities and offered to show us a few rooms. She was polite but did not invite us for an in-depth tour. It was clear to me that we were intruding and should have made an appointment. Like a naïve child, I never imagined that this place, which figured so prominently in my memories and mind, might have found a new identity and purpose.

From the front office, we went directly into the hallway leading to the former girls' ward. We stopped at the built-in storage shelves in front of the wide doorway. The woman said casually, "We use these shelves for storage, but no one here knows what their original purpose was." She opened the door to reveal a space filled with office and craft supplies.

I felt myself instantly become a small child in a line, waiting for bloomers.

"This is where the fresh linen was stored: the sheets and the bloomers and blouses we wore," I informed her.

"Oh," she remarked, a bit taken aback at my response. "That makes sense. Most of us know very little about the preventorium, other than it was a hospital for sickly children."

I had the sensation of my past being wiped away, casually erased. Time changes everything. She turned briskly, escorting us back to the hallway. I sneaked a glance behind us, back to the closed doors of the former sleeping ward where I had spent so many nights.

She next led us to one of the former classrooms, which we reached by going through the old Circle Room, now completely empty, and opened a door, saying, "This is the craft room, where our patients engage in a number of activities."

In the middle of the room six or seven oblong tables had been put together to form a rectangle. Sitting around them were men of all ages with multiple disabilities. As we stepped just inside the doorway, they all stopped their activities and stared at us, mouths open. The instructor clapped her hands and said, "Let's get back to work, everyone."

She didn't look at us or acknowledge our presence. I offered an inane smile, and we quickly backed out, feeling like we were intruders interrupting the flow of the day.

The doors leading to the dining room were closed, as was the back door leading down the concrete steps in the back where the playground had been.

We didn't ask and the attendant didn't offer a tour of the rest of the building. Instead, we hurried quickly back to the front offices, where the former living room had been. As we paused at the front door, I thanked her for showing us around. It was an awkward moment. I felt we had made a mistake just to show up and expect a grand tour with details. I could tell the woman was uncertain about how to communicate with us, though she was clearly trying to be polite. Ironically, I realized that we had interrupted the day's routine. I remembered how the nurses disliked disruptions in the routine. As we opened one of the front doors, she went to her desk drawer and pulled something out.

"Would you like a souvenir from the preventorium?" she called out to me. "I have a few of these and give them to those who occasionally come back to visit, like you."

Milk bottle

   She held out a small glass milk bottle. The top was covered with
a paper cap that read, MISSISSIPPI STATE SANATORIUM on it. I
held it, reading the carefully placed paper bottle cap. I remembered
these bottles well. Once again, I noticed that the word "preventorium" was nowhere on the bottle. It was not worthy of inclusion in
the building's history except as a memory of a place where sickly
children were nursed back to health. I wondered why on earth
I had thought to come here. I wished I had not come. My heart
felt cold and frozen. Could this really be the place I had spent so
many days? It felt unreal. Even the staff who now worked in the
building had only the vaguest knowledge of the preventorium. I
thought how we had interrupted their day. Perhaps some things
had not changed.
   But trying to be polite, I gripped the milk bottle and said,
"Thank you so much."

When we walked down the front steps, I turned to look back over my shoulder. I realized that there were now iron bars on every window on the first floor and that the columns had chipping plaster.

As we drove back to Jackson, neither my mother nor I said anything about what we had just experienced. We discussed our plans for the next day, our books, anything other the strange visit we had just made. I felt even more alienated from my past and fiercely questioned my memories.

Had I felt better or worse for having visited so abruptly and seeing the preventorium's transformation? Would it have been better to have simply remembered my time there, the bad and the good? Over the years, the humiliations and extreme routine had faded in my memory, but after this unplanned visit, I began to dream of them again vividly and regularly. This impulsive visit now also lurked in my memories. It was years before I visited again.

14

All the Children Gather

After my mother's death, I decided to once again to visit the preventorium. Through the Facebook group, the Magee Mississippi Preventorium, I had connected with many others who had also been patients there. The dates of our residence ranged from the 1940s through the closing of the facility in the mid 1970s. We shared photos and stories of our experiences, as well as scans of the newspaper articles that had featured the preventorium, state reports, the original daily schedule, and other materials. Most of all, we posted pictures with the question, "Do you remember me?"

We shared a universal need to be remembered, to have our time there validated, to confirm it had been real and that it mattered. Almost every one of us confided that upon returning home, no one mentioned the preventorium or talked about our time there.

As we conversed online, we shared the dates of when we had been patients. It was yet another way to validate our memories. One person responded to my photos saying I was in some of hers. We had been there at the same time. I recognized in another photo the little girl made to drink milk out of a baby bottle. None of us mentioned that—too painful. Not many of us remembered each other's names, but we did remember the names of the nurses and the director. As more stories and memories were shared, a clear division appeared. Some people had wonderful memories and had loved the staff. Some kept in touch with them after returning home. Others had horrible experiences and hated the staff. There seemed to be no in-between.

I was struck by the stark contrast in memories—either awful and traumatizing or entirely happy. Perhaps, in part, this was because children who came from more well-to-do families were more fortunate. Children who had visitors more often usually had a better experience.

People in the group occasionally organized small reunions in Magee.

The first reunion that I was attended took place in August 2018. As I flew to Mississippi, I felt a tightening in my chest and great trepidation. I borrowed a car from my brother, who lives in Madison, Mississippi, for the trip to Magee.

Although I was an adult, driving myself instead of a child sitting in the back seat of a 1950s car, I was much more nervous. I thought about that first trip to the preventorium and how, as a six-year-old, I had no knowledge of what I was about to experience.

South of Jackson, it felt as if I had stepped back in time. The silence of the humid heat and the overgrown forest threatening to take over the highway transported me back to my childhood. Highway 49 was now a separated four-lane highway instead of a lonely two-lane, but the forest, always thick and dense, still hovered close to the edge of the highway. Except for the odd ranch house set far back with a log fence around a huge green lawn, there was a feeling of emptiness. Every once in a while, I passed a large country farmhouse set up on a hill, cattle grazing in the fields close by.

I passed signs for Star, Mississippi, the Piney Woods School, and Mendenhall. They brought back memories of making up funny sentences in the car using town names, my mother murmuring while driving, saying the names out loud. In my childhood, these small towns seemed so distant from Jackson and so remote from any civilization. I never paid much attention to the actual places then, but I do now.

People seemed content to stay in their small towns, never even venturing to Jackson, the largest city in the state and only an hour away. It was discomforting. I have this same feeling in the Finger Lakes when I encounter people who have lived in the same small village all their lives and have only travelled a short distance from their home. Perhaps they lack the opportunity, desire, or the means to travel, but I immediately feel a sensation of smothering, of oppression in a place where not much seems to change, especially the people. Perhaps these feelings were a result of the isolation and routine at the preventorium. At least the Piney Woods School had changed. The lawns surrounding the school were gorgeously maintained, and they had a new sign, evidence of good care.

This 2018 reunion was scheduled around a grand celebration at the medical campus to celebrate one hundred years of the "Boswell Regional Center," as the entire medical facility and surrounding buildings was now called. The Boswell Regional Center is named for Dr. Boswell, who understood the grim future for those with tuberculosis.

The state had established the Boswell center in 1976, once the tuberculosis hospital closed. According to the website, it was established as one of five regional facilities in the state to treat those with "intellectual and developmental disabilities." The center's website explains that this medical campus is on the site of the original Mississippi State Tuberculosis Sanatorium. There is one brief—almost hidden—mention of the preventorium, where more than three thousand children spent time as patients.

I planned to meet the others who had come to the reunion at a local restaurant in Magee, right off Highway 49, in the middle of town. I was nervous and excited to be connecting in person with others whom I had only met online. One woman had been there the same time as me, but she had been older, aged nine to my age six, so we would not have really known or connected with each other.

As I drove into town, I realized with a jolt that fifty-nine years earlier, on this exact date in August of 1959, both she and I had been at the preventorium as patients. In all, there were four or five of us former patients at the reunion and one person who had been on staff just before it closed. The majority of us were women.

For an hour and a half, over lunch, we discussed how we had become patients at the preventorium and our experiences there. The stories we shared demonstrated some of the changes at the preventorium over the years. Some children from later years remembered swimming in a pool, more frequent family visiting days, and different nurses and teachers. Everyone remembered wearing bloomers, being barefoot, walking with arms akimbo, the milk we had to drink, the strict protocol for talking during mealtimes, and the "proper sleeping position."

There was an uncomfortable pause when someone asked me about why I had moved north. The person began to discuss Mississippi's racial history, making excuses for horrific behavior by saying there was also racial inequality in the North. This situation often occurred when I visited Mississippi. There is always a push and pull of guilt, denial, and realization of the truth. Even if it is not expressed, there is a shared understanding of the history of racial inequities. At this particular event, I did not want to engage but could not let the comments stand.

"We're here to talk about our experiences at the preventorium, not review the racist history of the state. This isn't the time or place."

The person responded angrily, beginning to defend the state's history, while the remainder of attendees at the table stared down at their laps mutely.

I interrupted, saying, "I love my home state, and I know there are people who are now trying to make things right, but the history cannot be denied or erased. I will not talk about this, but I will talk about our common histories together at the preventorium."

I have always struggled with the state's history, knowing the worst but also aware of others who were brave in the face of racism. I was surprised at my boldness. In the past, I would have hung my head meekly and said nothing, but that day I felt emboldened. I was tired of defending and explaining the North to the South when I was in Mississippi and also tired of trying to explain the best of Mississippi and the South to those in the North, which I now call home. I thought, too, that the anger came from a place of guilty understanding.

I began to ask the others at the table what they remembered most vividly about their time at the preventorium. They happily jumped in to smooth over the awkwardness.

"The stickers!" one woman shouted.

"Ice cream for all on Sunday afternoons!"

But the most common response was, "The bloomers!"

I had been too nervous to eat at lunch and had only had a tall, iced glass of southern "sweet tea." After the rest of the group had finished eating, the few of us who had met agreed to go to the old preventorium building for a tour. The reunion organizer had gotten approval for a tour for our group.

As we pulled out of the parking lot of Berry's Seafood Barn, which had the largest buffet of deeply fried anything I had ever seen, I somehow got separated from the others and had to find the preventorium alone. I preferred this anyway. I wanted to slow down and look at the Mississippi forests and the late-blooming black-eyed Susan flowers, to feel the extreme quiet of a deep summer day, and to savor the dense humidity and heat settling heavily on my skin. Time came to an almost frightening standstill when I was down South. It was so dense that everyone seemed to move in slow motion. It was a strange sensation. I felt my breath become labored even in the air-conditioned car.

After resetting the GPS navigation system twice, and going in two different directions, I decided to turn back north, towards Jackson, make a U-turn, and look for signs to Sanatorium. The GPS couldn't figure out "preventorium" but recognized "Sanatorium."

I finally found the Boswell Regional Center campus and turned onto a vast medical complex. In 1959–1960, this had been the tuberculosis sanitorium and preventorium on acres of beautiful lawns. It still retained beautifully manicured lawns but now had been expanded into multiple buildings to treat autism, mental health, and developmental disabilities. In my recollection, mental health and happiness were the least important aspect of life at the preventorium. No one thought about them. As children, we were supposed to follow directions. The focus was solely on physical health. Newspaper articles touted "happy children," which made all the adults feel better about a hospital where children were separated from their families. But it was far from the truth for many of us living day to day in the preventorium.

The campus had prepared for the hundredth anniversary celebration event. Parking lots were festooned with balloons on posts and had attendants to show the way. I stopped to talk with three different attendants to ask where the old preventorium building was located. The first young man seemed perplexed and told me he had never even heard that word. I thought to myself that it made sense, due to his youth. The next attendant, another young man, but a little older than the first, thought that I must be looking for the "kitchen" building, which was a renovated kitchen that had been moved to an older building, no longer in use. I explained that the preventorium had been a hospital for children and wouldn't have been turned into a kitchen. For just a moment though, I again doubted my memories: "Could it be a giant kitchen now?"

The third attendant I asked was a middle-aged woman. She thought a minute and said she did not know of it, but perhaps I was looking for the adult daycare center.

As I listened to her, I looked up into the distance. There, in front of me in stark relief, was the preventorium. Its façade looked exactly the same as it had fifty-nine years ago. I could see the circular driveway in front and the long sidewalk leading up to the columns and front portico. The scene looked like an old photo viewed through an antique stereoscope viewer. I felt a shiver along my spine.

That the people who worked on this campus knew nothing of the preventorium's very existence highlights how deeply buried its history has been. No wonder we all questioned our sanity and memories. No one ever wanted to talk about the preventorium except those who experienced it.

Looking over the attendant's shoulder, I felt as if I were looking at an old movie. I could almost see all the children as we walked on the front lawn.

I parked in a small lot off to the right where the others were waiting for me. We crossed the lawn, reminiscing aloud about our barefoot afternoon walks, pointing out to each other the "sticker patch." As we got closer, I noticed the building showed signs of wear and tear. There were deep gouges in the columns, peeling paint, and thick metal bars in all the outward-facing windows. A few of us posed for photos between the columns, now discolored and dun colored.

As we turned to enter the building, I saw that the gracious doorway had vanished. So too, sadly, had any semblance of the formerly elegant front room. As we stepped over the threshold, I looked down at the concrete floor of the portico. The deep red Cross of Lorraine, bold as ever, was still embedded in front of the door.

We clustered in the entryway which was now set up as office space, crammed with desks and cabinets, even more now than it had been when I made my earlier, ill-timed visit. The basic architecture remained, but the beautiful foyer/living room had been chopped up into shabby offices. The wall alcoves that once held vases of fresh flowers were empty concave spaces. The dark linoleum floor had been replaced, and as we walked slowly through the doorway into the hall, I saw that the hospital "sick room" where I had spent many nights alone and frightened was now a crowded office space with desks abutting one another. The girls' and boys' wards had become programming space. Every bit of space was in use but not necessarily well maintained, with grubby walls and floors. The wards themselves were smaller than I remembered.

The girls' ward was occupied by tables, desks, chairs, and people, some sitting by the windows, some at tables. Everyone welcomed us and generously offered a look around. Some of the patients waved to us or smiled; others turned their backs or went behind furniture to hide.

The floors and walls both needed a good cleaning and painting and there were bars in the windows on both sides. In the boys' ward, only one remaining window still had the special opening for lifting the window up to be latched to the high ceiling to allow air circulation. The old Circle Room was intact but now had painted metal benches set against the walls. There were three soft-drink machines against the walls. The former dining room and kitchen had been completely dismantled, and construction was underway with piles of lumber, plaster, and dirt. Our old classrooms were being used as craft rooms. This was the room I remembered from the time my mother and I had visited. The general impression was one of worn-out plaster, paint, and floors, a building needing maintenance that was outpacing the staff's ability to provide. I could hardly believe this was the same place.

As we made our way through the building, remembering and sharing memories of each room, I told the others about sneaking up the stairway to the director's apartment. They were shocked and reminded me that "no one was ever allowed to go upstairs." When we entered the preventorium, we all had retreated into "obedient" child behavior, and meekly asked for permission to take our short tour.

We continued into the main hallway. There was the stairway leading to the second floor with its curved wooden banister on our left. As I described how Ethel and I had crawled up the stairs, they all decided that we had to go up. The director's rooms were gone, replaced by another series of offices with chipping plaster on the walls. We found what would have been the bedroom and the famous closet, which now had a sturdy door and was used for storage.

Cross of Lorraine embedded at front entrance of preventorium

No evidence of the beautiful bedroom remained that I had admired forty-three years earlier. I heard someone behind me retelling the story of how I had sneaked up the stairs to look into the former director's closet and had viewed all her shoes. She was relaying the story to the woman whose office it was now. The staff member listened intently and then laughed at the story of children sneaking into the room to look at shoes. She laughed and asked us if we thought the building was haunted. She jokingly wondered if the ghost of the former director hurled shoes down the stairs and out the window at night. We stood still outside the office in a moment of silence. The preventorium was haunted for many of us while we were patients.

The group insisted taking photos of me on the stairway. It all looked much smaller at age sixty-five than at six years old. I remembered the hand-polished, curved, wood banister gleaming and the clean, sparkling stairs as I gazed through the balusters at the open apartment door, which led to the magic closet. My heart pounded as it did back then.

We wandered a little longer through the building, sharing memories of singing in the Circle Room, the television shows we had watched, and the holidays we spent there. We shared memories of our favorite foods and the ones we detested. We all remembered the bell, the napkin rings, and the center table with the gigantic flower arrangement.

As we drifted out the front door, we thanked the staff and stepped onto the Cross of Lorraine on the front portico overlooking the lawns, and all of us were silent, remembering.

15

Homecoming

I did not know that I was finally leaving the preventorium until the moment a nurse on the playground directed me to go inside, where another nurse was waiting for me with a stack of clothes.

"Susan," she said, "your mama is here. You need to go change clothes and then come with me to the living room."

Perhaps I was leaving again for a medical reason like I had when I had gone for a tonsillectomy. I had no reason to question the directions as I had learned not to question anything here. I changed into my clothes, a new white dress with a full skirt and lavender polka dots of all sizes.

"Leave your bloomers on the floor," the nurse directed me.

She took me by the hand, and we walked silently out of the girls' ward. My mother was standing at the front door with the director. At her feet stood the little suitcase we had brought a year and five months earlier. I ran to my mother, and she pulled me close. I buried my face in her skirt, hugging her legs.

"Come on, honey," she said to the top of my head. "We're going home."

Just a half hour ago, Ethel and I had been playing outside in the playgrounds, wandering and picking wildflowers to braid together for bracelets. She was teaching me how to mix daisies and black-eyed Susans together to make a flower chain bracelet. We had just gathered a bouquet when I heard my name and looked

Going home

up to see a nurse standing over us. When the nurse told me to go to the girls' ward, I didn't argue but stood up looking at Ethel: "I'll be back in a minute, and we can make our bracelets."

Now, standing next to my mother in my new clothes, I suddenly realized I was leaving. I asked if I was allowed to go say goodbye to Ethel, but the director said no. I never saw Ethel again.

"Oh, I will tell her you said goodbye," the director promised, smiling at me. "We'll keep in touch, Mrs. Currie. Let us know if you have any questions."

While I happily went with my mother to the car, delighted at being able to leave, I could not stop thinking of Ethel, on the playground waiting for me. I do not remember the trip home. According to my mother, I fell asleep in the front seat as we drove home, my head nestled close to her. I have a photo of me in that polka dot dress on the grounds of the preventorium on the day I left. I look uncertain and a bit woebegone. The suddenness of leaving was disconcerting even though I was happy to be with my mother. After being there for so long, one of the longer stays than usual, it was ironic that I had become so accustomed to life there that I felt jolted at the sudden change.

And I was upset and very sad that I had left my friend, Ethel, without saying goodbye. I was sad about this even as my beloved dog Tippy yipped and jumped all over me, licking my face. I sat in the backyard under a blooming mimosa tree and petted her. Tippy lay across my legs as if to keep me in place.

I asked my mother if I could write to Ethel to say goodbye, but she only smiled and said something along the lines of "Well, we'll see, but your grandmothers would love to have a letter from you." I never did send that letter to Ethel.

Years later, long after we were both grown, my brother told me that I had seemed very disoriented upon returning home from the preventorium. We hadn't lived in the Charleston Drive house for very long before I left, and I had not had time at to establish a routine there. For me, it was a brand-new house but to Ned, it was home; he and my mother had lived there for close to two years, most of it without me.

After the rigidity of the preventorium schedule, I had a difficult time adjusting to my new freedom. I often nervously waited for someone to direct or instruct me what activity to do next. Ned told me that I was strangely quiet.

"You had been living in a test tube," he said when describing his memories of that time. "It was difficult for you to become accustomed to the world again."

At an age when most children have learned to tell time, I had been stranded in a place where time had ceased to matter. For all of us at the preventorium, it was always "right now" and then on to the next scheduled activity. I never gained a proper sense of time. Minutes, hours, days blended together. I always worry there is something wrong with me when I don't respond to time in the same way as most people. But then I remember the flattening out of the days and the automation of my life at such a young age.

Soon after I returned home, my mother, brother and I went to visit family in Bogalusa, Louisiana, just north of New Orleans. I was outside wandering under the trees in their backyard when my cousin called me into the house for supper.

"I'll be there in a moment," I called back to him.

"A moment," he said mockingly. "You don't even know what a moment is."

"It's ninety seconds," I promptly responded. "I looked it up."

And I had looked it up. I needed to relearn how long a year was, a month, a week, a day, an hour, a minute, even a moment. I loved the word "moment" and understood intuitively that it was longer than a minute, something quite distinct. For many months after I came home, I thought about moments and what would constitute one moment at the preventorium. Time became an enigma to me, a challenge that I have to this day. From the extreme governing of time to abrupt freedom at home, it took a very long time to adjust.

When I returned home in August of 1960, it was just in time to be admitted into the second grade at Marshall Elementary School. Because I had only gone to school half days at the pre-ventorium, my mother met with the principal of the school and my second-grade teacher. Both were caring, compassionate people who truly believed in what they were doing for children. They worked with my mother so that I could attend class until noon. As everyone else was preparing to go to lunch in the cafeteria, the principal would appear in the doorway to my classroom. He and my teacher would pull me aside to ask if I wanted to stay the entire day in the classroom. For several weeks, I said, "No, I want to go home."

The principal personally walked me most of the way home, which was about ten or fifteen minutes away through a neighborhood and small park. He was a cheerful man with a crewcut who was always joking with the children and making us laugh. We all loved him. We loved to say his name out loud as it had a wonderful sound when shouted.

"Mr. Hooper!" we would yell when we saw him. He always smiled and waved.

On the way home, we would stop at the bridge in the tiny park, and I would shout over the water, "Mr. Hooper, Mr. Hooper is walking me home!"

After the first couple of times, he joined me in shouting this over the stream.

At the park, our babysitter, Gladys, met us and then the principal would return to school. I enjoyed this special attention and felt unique among all my classmates.

I soon formed my first close friendship with a little girl in my class who lived down the street from me and gradually adjusted to a full day of class. The principal and teacher no longer checked in with me at noon. But I still remember the teacher and the principal helping me readjust. It also helped my mother. She was a widow who had no choice but to go to work every day. She worried if I would make it through the full day at school.

As late as the third grade, I was still feeling the effects of the extreme routine at the preventorium. One day the teacher asked me to announce that it was noon and time for lunch. I said instead, "Who decided that it is twelve o'clock? How do we really know what time it is?"

The teacher, without missing a beat, nodded at me, told me to be seated and called on another child to announce the time. But she sent me home with a note asking to meet with my mother. When I gave my mother the note, she sighed after reading.

"Honey, why didn't you say what time it was? You know how to tell time."

I thought of the preventorium for a minute. Then I responded. "Because there is no time," I said defiantly. "There is only right now!"

"Oh Lordie," she replied in a tired voice. "Sometimes I just don't know . . . but if you will just mind the teacher, say what time it is, we will go to the library and get books about time."

We did go to the library to learn about time. But I never told my mother that in addition to God and Santa, I no longer believed in time. I didn't have the words to explain what a foreign concept it was to me since the preventorium. There, time was measured simply by morning, midday, afternoon, sunset, and night; or breakfast, dinner, and supper; or bath time, playtime, and school. I now had to learn to adapt to a different system to function. I understood the need for the construct of time, but it was never a clear and easy system for me.

Meals, among the most regimented times at the preventorium, were strange for me once I returned to school. I was used to no loud talking, raucous laughter, or long conversations.

At my elementary school, I was surprised at the variety of food in the cafeteria, where we might have a chance to choose between two vegetables or even to bring our own lunches in a lunchbox. My mother had bought me a lavender and pink lunch box with a ballerina in a white tutu embossed on the front. And everyone at the table talked to each other constantly, talking over each other, laughing, giggling, exchanging parts of their lunches with each other.

At the preventorium, the food was good for our health, but the rigor and stern discipline made us dislike it. I swore secretly to myself that I would never have milk or eggs once I returned home.

I once asked my mother and brother if they wanted to see me drink an entire glass of milk in a short amount of time. Thinking they were being supportive, they both said yes enthusiastically. I quickly drank down a juice glass of milk as quickly as I could. Then I put it down on the table and informed them, "There, that is the last glass of milk I will ever drink!"

Neither reacted at first. They weren't sure if I was making a joke. My mother just nodded and said, "Good for you for drinking that milk."

For a while, she put out a glass for me at every meal, but I never touched it. She eventually gave up. I was too young to have the words to communicate how the full butterfat milk had disgusted me and ruined any enjoyment of milk ever again. Even when we visited our grandparents in Parchman, Mississippi, where full butterfat milk was delivered to their door every two to three days, and we all, myself included, begged our grandmother to have a turn churning the butter in the glass jar churn that had a hand-cranked handle, I never took a sip of the milk itself. If I happened to catch a whiff of it, I had to stifle my gag. The memory was too vivid of having to suck up the remnants of full-fat milk from the preventorium milk bottles, proudly bearing the 4.5 percent butterfat on the "State Sanitorium Buttermilk"–labeled paper caps or the small glasses brought around midafternoon.

After the preventorium, I rarely slept through an entire night and still do not to this day. For the entire first year home, I slept with my mother. After being in a ward with fifteen to twenty other girls, I could not accommodate to sleeping in a small bedroom alone in the dark. My mother was patient and never reprimanded me, although I know it must have been interrupted sleep for her too, as I would wake in the night, tossing and turning.

Once home, I wandered aimlessly around our house at night, unable to sleep. I loved that I could get out of bed whenever I wanted, freed from the strict eyes of watchful nurses.

In addition, I had "personal hygiene" issues once the strict schedule for bathroom breaks ended. I suffered numerous kidney infections due to my inability, uncertainty, and confusion about when to go to the bathroom. I had imposed my own limited schedule for bathroom breaks.

For years, I struggled to adapt to my family's unfamiliar routine and to mingle with neighborhood children who saw me as "other.

To them, I had, one day simply been whisked away and then just as suddenly returned.

Years later, I asked my mother if she had received any instructions for my homecoming.

"None," she told me. "They just told me to go back to a normal schedule."

But there was no normal schedule, for neither me nor my brother and mother. They had created a new separate routine while I was away. Now, I had to accommodate to another completely unfamiliar schedule. The fifteen months I spent at the preventorium had erased any and all normal household patterns I might have had. I felt I had turned a corner into another dimension upon my arrival at the preventorium, and then, unexpectedly, I took another turn around a corner thrust me into my mother's and brother's established routine as an outsider and a stranger.

◆ ◆ ◆

Even today I find myself often walking in single file with my arms akimbo, hands on my waist. I continued this habit long after I returned home from the preventorium. Friends found this odd and asked why. For years, I couldn't or wouldn't remember and always replied, "It's more comfortable this way." Teenage years were torture because it made me too "different," but I could not change the habit. It was only after reconnecting with former patients that I recalled our single-file walks with hands at our waists.

To this day, at least once a night, if not more often, I wake to find myself in "the proper sleeping position," on my back, hands by my sides and my head turned toward the door. Sometimes I have my hands crossed one over the other on my chest, which was also a habit I formed at the preventorium. It doesn't matter where I am—at home or in a hotel—somehow, my head intuitively turns toward the door when I am sleeping. I wake and wonder where I am, even if I am at home. For a moment, I look for the whiteness

of the sheets, the white wall, and the white uniforms and shoes
of the nurses, before I realize where I actually am.

I always, *always* sit on the edge of a chair with my feet planted
flat in front of me, sitting up as straight as I can. As a child, a
university student, and as an adult, when working and attending
meetings, no matter the type of chair, I find myself in this posture,
feet on the floor, alert and ready for action.

In times of stress, I hold my hand on my chest just under my
throat and swing my body side to side. I often wake in the night
tapping my lower lip and wriggling my right foot as I did to fall
asleep at the preventorium.

Dining is also always a formal affair for me. I cannot easily
attend informal gatherings where we hold a plate in our hands
or lap. Sitting on the ground to eat is nearly impossible for me.
Even when completely alone, I sit at the table with a place setting
that is just so.

Washing my face is always done with the washcloth folded in
a square, with its very ends dipped under the water to be wetted.

I am very good at queuing up in line for anything—grocery-store
checkout, movie tickets, voting. I spent every day for a year and
a half at a formative age doing so.

Nor do I wonder about the disappearance of people and friends
in my life. I understand that it will happen all the time. This can
seem like coldness on my part but early on, I learned that loss is
inevitable. Safety is an illusion.

Taking a daily nap is a requirement that has been difficult to
fulfill most of my adult working life.

Daydreaming, letting my mind wander and having the ability
to appear as though I am listening when I am not, are skills I per-
fected in the preventorium. I sometimes have a long conversation,
in which I appear to have listened carefully but in fact, remember
very little of what was said, as I am in my own world of thoughts.

I still do not like eggs or milk in plain form and only tolerate
them with a great amount of modification in things like quiche

or ice cream. I cannot abide egg custard, rice pudding, cabbage, or okra in any form.

I still have extreme insomnia and wait hours for the dawn to return.

And two or three times every night I go to a window to search for a light in a house somewhere, anywhere, to prove I am not the only one awake in the night.

◆ ◆ ◆

The majority of records detailing our daily routine and time as patients at the preventorium are lost. Additionally, memories of the preventorium movement, once so prevalent across the country, have all but faded into oblivion. How does a medical movement, a significant one, become lost to memory? How does it get forgotten? Not until someone uncovers a long-lost photo, found by accident in an old album? Until one person with unwanted and untrusted memories that rise up during sleepless hours decides to explore fact and fiction and to seek out others with the same experience?

What was on the numerous clipboards that the nurses kept? They wrote down on charts every single thing we did, from eating and sleeping to bathroom habits, every single day. Even while we were outside playing, the nurses and aides were watching us and taking notes. They were in the classrooms during classes, studying us as if we were experiments to be tracked. But none of us children, at least no one that I ever knew, saw a chart up close. What exactly was on them?

Most of us remember the personal hygiene record keeping, as we all felt the invasion of privacy and the humiliation of having to tell the nurse about our bowel movements in front of others. And if we were unable to "perform," we had the added insult and punishment of having to stay in the bathroom until we got results. Many jokingly called the morning clipboards, the "poop" records. I hated this term and tried not to listen to the jokes. We all shared the shame.

I do not remember clipboards at meals, but meals must have been recorded. My mother knew all about my "pickiness" and refusal to eat and encouraged me to finish meals when she visited. The nurses always kept her updated. And there were records of weight gains and losses.

As a sickly, asthmatic child, I was often in the preventorium's hospital "sick room," especially during the first six months of my residence. There was, of course, a clipboard at the end of the bed that the nurse and doctor used when checking on me.

Did they record the hysterical crying fit that I had when, due to bronchitis, I had to miss the story of Rapunzel on *Walt Disney*? Did they record the shot they gave me to calm me down when I had cried myself into a full-blown asthma attack after begging them not to leave me alone in the dark sickroom?

Over three thousand children passed through the Mississippi Preventorium in the more than forty years it existed. I imagine a room of filing cabinets with paper charts stuffed so tightly in each drawer that extricating one would be almost impossible.

Our health records filed at the Mississippi State Health Department were not informative. When many of us former patients requested our records from the preventorium, we were shocked to see that the records were mostly blank except for first and last names, date of birth, weight upon arrival, and weight upon leaving.

I had completed the request form and received a call from a lovely and polite young woman at the Mississippi Heath Department. She asked some questions about the preventorium, as she had not known of its existence.

"I will conduct a search for your records and call you if there are any questions," she told me.

Several weeks later, she called again. She addressed me, "Miss Susan," which caught me off guard. I had not expected to hear this old southern way of addressing older women.

"Miss Susan, I did a preliminary search," she said in her soft accent, "and I need to ask you a few more questions. May I ask what your maiden name is?" I was charmed by her sweet manners.

And I was momentarily taken aback. I had forgotten that in the South, a woman almost always took her spouse's last name and gave up her maiden name. She must have thought that my last name on the request form was my married name. I had checked the "Married" spot on the form.

"Currie is my maiden name," I responded politely. "I kept my name."

"Oh!" She was clearly very surprised. "Oh, I see."

I was shocked to realize that the old southern ways were still in full force for women. I should not have been surprised. It is one of the numerous reasons I left my home state, even though there are so many things about it that I love and appreciate, such as the courtesy and exquisite manners.

"Now, Miss Susan," she said, and I could tell from her voice that she was smiling, "I believe that your records, like so many others, must be kept somewhere at the Boswell Regional Center. We just don't have your records here. I have looked and looked."

I had already called the Boswell main office and knew that the old records were not there. Keeping records for all the children who had been patients at the preventorium was just not a priority. After so many decades, old medical records from long-retired pediatricians had surely been destroyed.

On social media, we former patients wonder not only what was on those countless charts but also what happened to them.

Lost, tossed, not considered important?

Copies of our records should be in the state health department, but they are not. Perhaps they were sent to our home doctors who are now long dead and their records purged.

16

A Complicated and Fierce Woman

My mother was a complicated woman: incredibly smart but not educated beyond high school, fiercely independent, and protective of her children. She was sometimes suspicious and harsh in her views and suffered from low self-esteem. Though she accepted bad behavior from people in a higher socioeconomic class and resented it too, she craved recognition and beauty and coped with difficulties through her deep religious faith.

Born in 1927 in rural New Hebron, Mississippi, she was the third child of four. Smaller than her brother and two sisters, who were all tall with dark, almost black hair, she was petite with white-blonde hair. She was smart, imaginative, and different from her family. She had undiagnosed dyslexia and was shy and unsure of herself. Growing up during the Depression was difficult in an extremely poor and rural part of the state. My grandfather had a small farm, and everyone in the family had chores. My mother helped with animals and gardens, cooking and cleaning. It was a rough, hard-scrabble world. I have a very old, faded photograph of her, smiling, as a teenager standing over her favorite black pig, which had one white ear and a white face. The farm was sold shortly after the photo was taken, and her family moved to Jackson, where she went to high school, graduated, and found a job at a local department store.

Throughout our lives, our mother told my brother and me about growing up in the country. She wanted us to understand

and accept her rural southern accent and her "country ways," as she called them, and her family. She needed her rural experience to matter to us, and though she could not articulate it, she needed us to understand her childhood and where she had come from. She needed and wanted to matter, to have an impact on our lives.

For as long as I could remember, she loved telling stories about the farm, where she wandered alone in the forests near the house, dreaming of fairies resting in flowers but also working the land with her family. As an adult, remembering her tales, I thought of my time at the preventorium, looking for fairies among the wildflowers. She possessed encyclopedic amounts of knowledge about plants, gardening, herbs, cooking, canning, and nature but was very modest and became uncomfortable with being the center of attention, even though she secretly craved the recognition.

The holidays were a time of joy for her, cooking her mother's recipes, baking, and making fancy dishes for us. She told me how, one Christmas during the Depression, her father traveled all afternoon by bus to the coast to bring back a barrel of fresh oysters on ice to be shared with the neighbors for the evening holiday feast.

But other stories were melancholy. She spoke of the loneliness of weekend afternoons, feeling she was the last person on earth in that desolate, poor farm country. She looked into the distance as she told me of the isolation, listening for any sound at all to prove she was not totally alone.

"Oh, let me be not alone," she thought.

Sometimes she stayed home from Sunday-night church, to make sure the animals were fed, watered, and in their pens for the night. She was the only person on the farm—even the animals were quiet. She stood "stock still," watching the moon and stars rise.

"Just me," she said, "and the sun sinking lower and lower until twilight was over . . . and then the frogs and crickets would begin their conversations. I used to wander the farm in the gloaming, looking for a light in the distance, listening for a human sound or a car out on Highway 49, even though I knew that was too far to hear anything. But I never saw any or heard anything, we were so isolated in New Hebron."

I always loved the name of that tiny town. It sounded so biblical. I loved hearing her say the word "gloaming" in her soft, rural, southern accent.

She always talked of the gloaming. That feeling of isolation at dusk stayed with her all her life and intensified after my father died. Every twilight, she felt especially alone and imagined every household having purpose except for her.

Many years later, when she was quite elderly, she lived in a nursing home in Mississippi. I had decades ago moved north to Ithaca, New York, a move that was difficult for her because I was so far away. I tried to mitigate the distance between us by calling her every day, especially on Sunday evenings, which were more difficult for her as she imagined happy families preparing for the week ahead. And I returned to visit her as often as I could, more often as she aged.

One Sunday afternoon, on one of our last visits, we went to my brother's house for supper. She enjoyed sitting in the big kitchen, listening to us getting caught up on family news. Every so often, she would interrupt to issue instructions for meal preparation or to correct a memory. Mostly, she just watched and smiled.

After dessert, sharing more memories, it was time to take her back to the nursing home. My brother and I helped her into her wheelchair and took her out to the car. It was a Sunday night in late March. It was early spring in the warm South, where flower fragrances explode into the soft heat at night.

As we pushed the wheelchair to the car, chatting, she suddenly exclaimed, "Y'all hush for a minute."

We both paused and watched her as she looked up intently into the sky.

"Look—there's the moon and stars!" she cried out delightedly. "I haven't seen the moon in a long, long time."

We stood silently for a while, watching the sky grow darker and the crescent moon grow brighter.

"Ah...," she sighed with great satisfaction, "ah...the gloaming."

♦ ♦ ♦

As a child, I did not ask my mother many questions about my time at the preventorium once I was home. Questions brought on awkward silences and sometimes even anger. Her first response to any question was, "I didn't have a choice. The doctor said you would die if I didn't take you there." She was angrily defensive when I brought it up. "It was hard on Ned and me, too."

After a while, I stopped asking. I understood that it was an emotional land mine. Oh, how I wish I had her asked what she and my brother did while I was away.

Did my mother and brother miss me, talk about me? Was my conversation at the dinner table missed? Did they feel my absence? What was their regular routine? I know my mother worried about me, scared that I might be unhappy, afraid, or lonely.

When she visited me at the preventorium, she asked me questions, but I instinctively knew I had to make her feel better. And I wanted to make her feel better. She was so sad each time she saw me, I laughed and told her how much fun I was having with all these boys and girls to run about with and to have as friends. But I did not feel it was fun at all—not the kind of lighthearted fun I wanted to have during summer months, swimming, reading at all hours, gazing up at the stars at night. I felt and was alone among strangers there.

What did Ned think or feel about my absence? Did he wonder what I was doing? Did he wish I were home? When we spoke about my time at the preventorium, he told me that he often asked, "When is Susan coming home?"

While at the preventorium, I tried to picture his daily routine. He and my mother would have breakfast together and then go to pick up Mary, our beloved caretaker. My mother would drive Mary to the house. Ned would walk to elementary school, and Mary would meet him at the end of the school day. I heard him telling Mary about his day. Then he would pet Tippy and play with her in the back yard.

When my mother came home, she hugged Ned and chatted with Mary. After taking Mary home, she and Ned would catch up on the day. Perhaps she read while he did homework, or they would watch TV together. After my brother went to bed, my mother had a little time to herself to prepare for the next day. On Saturdays, I wondered if they went to the zoo or the movies or if they made cookies together. Did she attend my brother's baseball games? I wanted to imagine their conversations but could not. I only heard silence, or perhaps it was my own silence I heard.

On Sunday mornings, I saw them dressing in their best clothes for Sunday school and church. My brother would wear a white shirt and tie. My mother wore a suit or a pretty dress. She carried short, wrist-length white gloves with tiny seed pearls around the edges, wore a small hat with tiny feathers and a short veil. I remembered how cozy and safe, after the cold church pews, it felt to crawl into the sun-warmed back seat of our car and how I lay there listening to my mother and brother talk on the way home.

On the Sundays my mother visited me, I thought that she and Ned would have had a light lunch before she made the hour drive south to Magee, Mississippi, to the preventorium. On the Sundays she did not visit, I imagined the big Sunday dinner they would have for just the two of them. Perhaps my grandparents or an aunt, uncle, and cousins invited them for a visit. But in reality, I never knew what my mother and brother did or said or felt while I was at the preventorium. I was confused after I returned home when someone referred to an event or a family outing that had happened while I was away. I had lost contact with everyone. I was a stranger in my own family and home.

What did my brother do when my mother visited me? Were there siblings of other children in the preventorium outside the permitted perimeter? Did he interact with them? Years later, my mother admitted it had been hard on him to visit the preventorium. When he could not accompany my mother, where did he go? Was he with aunts and uncles or neighbors, or did my mother pay someone to stay with him?

Many years later, my brother and I had the first conversation of our lives about the preventorium. We both wondered why, in over a lifetime, neither of us had raised the topic. He was trying to be sensitive to my feelings, and I was too ashamed of the experience. I asked him what he remembered. He described how our mother told him that I had to go away to "build up my strength." She told him that I had anemia and a weak body.

I was shocked to learn that he had made the trip to the preventorium *every single time* my mother came to visit! All these years and I had not known this. I had never known that he was on the preventorium grounds while she visited with me. Here we were on visiting Sundays, so close and yet so far apart, divided by lawns, buildings, and regulations. I only remember one time seeing him at a distance. He remembers that, too, as he had been wandering by the parking lot and wandered over close to the playgrounds. Our mother brought me to the edge of the invisible boundary separating those who could be close to the preventorium children and those, like him, who could not. He waved and I waved wildly to him with both of my arms over my head.

On visiting Sundays, he told me that he and our mother would go to church as I imagined. Afterwards, they had lunch and then drove to Magee.

Like me, Ned has vivid memories of the trip down Highway 49 to the preventorium. He remembers the signs for "Piney Woods" and a famous furniture store where rocking chairs were made.

"Memory is a tricky thing," he told me. "One fills in the little details and things."

He is correct about memory. Sometimes I do not know if I have actually remembered something real or if I heard the story so many times that I think I remember it.

The red brick of the buildings made a strong impression on him. I was stunned to hear that his memories match my own. I have often felt that the stark red buildings on lush grounds are tattooed on my inner eyelids.

While my mother was visiting me, my brother was on his own, he told me. He was eight years old, wandering around the preventorium and sanitorium grounds, exploring every empty building. He said, "I tried to open every door I found."

He roamed the grounds and found doors that opened into vacant sections of the TB hospital. These were different from the main TB hospital and preventorium. These were one-story, blond-brick buildings with empty hospital rooms, joined by a corridor down the center. This abandoned part of the hospital was not in disrepair, just oddly empty and abandoned. He wandered down corridor after corridor, looking into empty room after empty room, noting that they were in relatively good shape. As he went through the empty, deserted wards, looking for something to occupy him, he stopped often to glance nervously behind him. The isolation and emptiness of the rooms were spooky and unsettling.

He saw almost no one during his rambles on the grounds. If he did encounter an adult, he recalled our mother's instructions: "Never talk to any strangers!"

At the first sight of any adult, he hid behind one of the massive trees on the grounds, peering around it until the person had safely passed.

I asked him what he did during the unusually cold winter that I was there.

He didn't especially remember the winter but does remember vividly the books he read while waiting in the car for my mother. Reading and books were a big part of our home life, and we both have strong, specific memories of books.

He read the *Iliad*, even though he was only eight years old, and the *Aeneid*. He read them over and over. We both had been taught to read early by our father, and we both loved mythology so I wasn't surprised to hear these were his favorites. There were editions of these books on our bookshelves at home.

He told me that one Sunday afternoon, he tried to read a copy of Thomas More's *Utopia* which he found on a shelf. It had been one of our father's books. But he could not understand it and put it back on the shelf. We both remember *Under Drake's Flag* by G. A. Henty. This is the book, he said, that made him become fascinated with England and English history. We both loved the biography series The Childhood of Famous Americans by the Bobbs-Merrill Company, with distinctive orange covers. We devoured these, taking armfuls from our church library every Sunday after I had returned home from the preventorium.

At our young ages, the two-hour visits every other Sunday could have felt interminable, but Ned was caught up in the books he brought with him, many of which he has still.

He described another haunting memory while wandering the preventorium grounds. Once, he remembers sneaking as close to the edge of the playground as he could, near a back corner of the preventorium building but still far away from the groups of people he could see.

Grownups, dressed in their Sunday best were standing around in little clumps, visiting. Children, dressed in nothing but white cotton bloomers were darting about and running all over and through the groups of adults. Between the overly dressed adults and the skinny, practically naked, frail-looking children, the contrast was stark and shocking. The children reminded him of cygnets, baby swans moving swiftly among the adults. He was at a distance, and he could not tell the boys from the girls. It was a surreal view and he never forgot it.

How strange that our family was geographically in one place but not together. And our mother had to leave one child unattended to see the other. In the back of her mind, she must have been wondering where he was, what he was doing, and if he was safe. Our visits were only two hours or so, so perhaps she did not worry. I cannot remember her leaving me to go check on him.

When I returned home, it was as if the preventorium didn't happen, like a time lapse in a science-fiction story. Only I knew the facts of my experience. And yet, I could not articulate clearly just what that experience had been, nor did anyone want to hear about it. It was not just my mother and brother but also friends and extended family. It was an awkward and difficult topic to discuss. In those days, we did not address any of these kinds of extreme situations. It was also not considered socially acceptable to discuss it. We had language for describing physical illness but not emotional trauma.

We let the memories fade—or hoped they faded away.

When I returned, I had a difficult time connecting with the world. I had to relearn the routine social norms and behaviors of everyday social interactions. I was silent and did not fit in well. I imagine that, in some ways, I was like a prisoner released into sudden freedom. I do not remember specifics, but my brother confirms my disorientation continued for quite a while without the routine of the preventorium.

I had assumed my brother was fine with my absence, but he also suffered the shock of separation. First, he suffered the loss of our father, then we were uprooted from our old house and neighborhood, and finally, I disappeared. He was often afraid in the night and frequently went to my mother for reassurance.

We were both suffering from these separations in similar ways but did not know it until many years later.

When I returned home, he taught me cursive writing and was delighted the first time I awkwardly wrote my first and last names. We had a number of adventures together while in elementary school, the most memorable being when we invented our own type of Morse code. Home from school, sick, in bunkbeds in his room, we worked all afternoon perfecting our system for "Yes," "No," and other vital words. When our mother came home from work, she asked us a question, we responded with our system of taps on the wall. After a number of tapping responses, she cried out to us, "Y'all talk to me, stop knocking on the wall!"

We giggled and kept tapping.

While I was away at the preventorium, our mother bought a swing set and swimming pool for the backyard. We remember a memorable neighborhood pool party after my return, turning our backyard into a vast patch of mud and killing all the grass my mother had planted the previous weekend. In 1978, when my mother sold the house, the rusting swing set was still there. My brother and I spent hours seeing how high we could swing on that set.

◆ ◆ ◆

I thought often about the preventorium, but it was not until late middle age that I actively began to look for information.

When I did begin research, in the one book and few articles I found, preventoria were presented as institutions for "poor people." The poor were presumed to be unable to care for their children. Were we poor? We lived in a modest, middle-class neighborhood. My mother sometimes struggled financially, but we had plenty of food, clothing, and all our necessities. We had numerous gifts at birthdays and holidays.

Sometimes, information about my time there came from surprising situations. One was the time I took my mother for a visit to New York City. I had made an appointment to interview her for StoryCorps, a program to capture the voices of everyday people. The interviews are archived at the Library of Congress. My mother had made difficult decisions about her children and life. She had worked so hard with so few comforts, opportunities, or privileges in life, other than being white. I wanted her to talk about the years on her family's farm before they moved to Jackson, where she met my father. I planned to duplicate the CD and give it as a gift to my brother and his children.

In the interview, my mother's "down home" charm, her lilting, soft, rural southern accent and natural wittiness came to the fore. She told a story about a bus trip to the Gulf Coast, where she asked her father for a Dr. Pepper soft drink. A woman on the bus, cried out, "Who is asking for pepper on such a hot day!" The recording attendant stifled her giggles. My mother recounted stories about World War II, about seeing her brother in uniform in the movie newsreels at the local cinema and how she and her sisters ran home to tell their mother. She told riveting stories about the Great Depression and her high school years.

But her words about me as a child were, "You were so difficult." I couldn't believe I had heard her correctly. I believed I was the obedient child who never caused her one second of worry. My brother was adventurous, eager for new experiences, and some-times rebellious. They had argued often when he was in high school. I must have looked shocked. She hastily explained that I was difficult only because I was sickly and wouldn't eat. And then she had to send me to the preventorium. My heart throbbed with emotion, but I said nothing. I kept the recording but never had copies made. I couldn't bear for my family to hear her say, "You were so difficult." I understood she meant a particular moment in time, just before I went to the preventorium, but was that her primary memory of me? Not the years when I endlessly tried to help make life easier for her by taking care of the cleaning, the laundry, and as much cooking as I could?

Once on a visit to Jackson for research, she said abruptly to me, "You were being taken care of—your poor brother had it worse. He had to sit and wait while I visited you. And at Christmas, you got all those gifts."

"Your memory is wrong," I shot back. "At the preventorium, children were allowed one gift each and at the end of the visit, the gift went home with the visitors."

She was still for a minute. Then she acknowledged I was correct. But my heart was in my throat and I felt the pain of this exchange. Why were anger and frustration her first and only response to anything I said about the preventorium? How could she have abandoned me at the preventorium and then assumed all was well? Was it because I had tried to make it easy for her by being cheerful and happy? Why didn't she see through my ruse?

My mother always loved me, but even when I was very small, she saw me as a responsible adult and expected me to act alike one. I tried so hard to appear happy and well-adjusted while I was at the preventorium. I did not want to worry her. This, understandably, led her to believe I was happy there, and yet, even when I tried to talk about my experience, she could not hear it.

Were there echoes for her of her own lonely, isolating experience as a bright, imaginative child on a farm in the deep country? Was it too painful for her to wonder if I had been as alone at the preventorium as she had felt in her childhood?

Once, while taking her on a special trip to England, we stayed at Borthwick Castle outside of Edinburgh. On the first evening, along with the other guests, we attended a formal dinner in the grand dining room. A long banquet table had been set with exquisite and elegant candelabras, fine china, crystal, and silver. We were dressed in our finest "Sunday clothes," as my mother described them. During the cocktail hour before dinner, we mingled with the other guests. My mother was a popular guest. Everyone was delighted with her exotic accent and her Mississippi origins. It was a place so far away and unknown to the mostly British guests. They had heard of the Mississippi River but had never before met anyone who lived in the state.

At the dinner table, during conversations amongst the guests, I was startled to overhear my mother say to the woman next to her, "My daughter went to the preventorium because she was so sickly. She would have died if she hadn't gone." That was the only phrase

I heard. But I caught a glimpse of the woman's face, inquisitive and intently listening.

Why did my mother confide to a stranger when she wouldn't talk to me? Had the woman shared her own medical story, and in return, had my mother felt compelled to share my story? I've often wondered what was in my mother's mind. I never learned the details of the remainder of that conversation.

My brother thought that our mother had little self-awareness and that this was a saving characteristic. She was a widow in the late fifties compelled to work, who established a home, took care of her children, and had to be independent and self-sufficient at a time when strong women, especially widows, were viewed with suspicion. There was a belief that they were after other women's husbands. My mother was relentless in protecting us and even turned down two marriage proposals that would have made her life much easier because, as she said, "I couldn't allow anyone other than me to tell my children what to do. That is my job."

Over the years, I continued to try to engage with my mother about the preventorium, but she was alternately defensive, judgmental of me, or focused on how awful it was for her and my brother.

Her reaction was rooted in guilt and shame. She felt inadequate as a mother because I was ill and in the hospital so often after my father's death. Now I know how horrible those years must have been for her.

Decades after his death, we had heard accidentally from a great uncle about our father's condition at the hospital. As our uncle began saying something about "Ed living in that condition," my mother stopped him, saying in a stern voice I had never heard, "There are some things my children do not need to know. They do not need that burden." My brother and I looked at each other. My brother and I had not known this or exactly what happened. We only knew that he had lived a week, then died. We did not ask our mother about it.

It was her secret to keep.

The preventorium was another sore spot too. The doctor had insisted the preventorium was the only option for bringing me back to health.

Now I understand how much more was embedded in the year before I was sent to the preventorium. The endless nights that my mother took care of my brother and me while working full-time, her sadness and courage as she tried to carry on, her desperate efforts to keep me healthy, and my many times hospitalized.

I have often wondered if the doctor sent me to the preventorium because he knew that, in my mother's grief, she could not manage both my brother and me. Did she feel that she had to choose between us?

She often expressed impatience and anger at me for not being grateful. In her mind, I had been taken care of at the preventorium, but in her anger, there was hidden shame that she had to send me there as well. What must it have been like at, age twenty-nine, to be left without her beloved husband, who lifted her up every day with his love, who was her anchor in unfamiliar social situations, and who had contributed in so many ways to a happy life and home? She had two small and needy children and a family who was not as helpful as they might have been. All of this must have been overwhelming.

And yet, she managed brilliantly. Our father had taken out a life insurance plan, of course, never expecting to die so young. Using $10,000 from the plan, our mother put a down payment on a small, three-bedroom ranch house on Charleston Drive, in a new subdivision still under development. Her business and financial skills allowed her to do much with little. When we were both in junior high school, she stopped employing sitters. She told us we were grown up enough to come home and behave while she was at work. We had to call her as soon as we were home every day to let her know we were there. While this must have been worrying for her, it taught us independence and accountability. During this same time, she took on a second part-time job as financial manager for a highly regarded local department store. She worked two jobs until she turned sixty-five, then retired from the full-time job and kept the thirty-hour-per-week position as financial manager until she was in her seventies. She insisted that we go to college, something she was never able to do for herself.

Mothers often act more confidently than they feel with their children, to demonstrate strength. My mother, in particular, felt she had to present herself as strong and flourishing. If she showed vulnerability, it brought forth unwelcome advice to remarry or to "get some help" with raising the children. Even as a small child, I could see through my mother's brave façade. My mother was unusual. She bought a car and a house and cared for us. She carried the load of two parents.

When she visited me at the preventorium, she was not with her children together. Her guilt over this, with one child a patient, the other on his own during visits, made her defensive. She had to make it okay somehow that I had been left in this strange hospital and not at home with her and my brother.

I wish I had reassured her in the end that all ended well at the preventorium. For all the negative experiences at the preventorium, I learned how to rely upon myself and how to function in the world. I developed self-sufficiency and resiliency. And my brother grew up to be a brilliant, kind, and generous man.

Even though my mother could never speak about the preventorium, I understood that she felt it was a failure of hers as a mother. But in the end, my physical health did improve significantly.

She saved my life with this difficult and painful decision.

17

Lasting Impressions

For more than sixty years, I have been trying to make sense of the preventorium and my experiences there. For so many years, I buried in my memory this shameful secret that I never shared and that my family never discussed. I was conflicted about the place and my experience. Yes, it did improve my physical health and the physical health of so many other children. But I was also emotionally traumatized and haunted by the experience.

I cannot speak for every child who was a patient, but I harbor so much shame from the preventorium: shame at feeling "other" and at being considered deficient and different; shame in always being linked to tuberculosis, which none of us contracted; shame of being from such an impoverished state, which had the highest death rate from tuberculosis in the nation, particularly among the Black population; shame of being white while many other "at risk" children of color may have not been taken care of at all.

Ironically, in 1953, the Magee tuberculosis hospital was rated the best in the nation. The article "Tops in the Nation," which appeared in *Carraway's Store and Theatre News*, published in Prentiss, Mississippi, highlighted the initiative of Dr. Henry Boswell in obtaining the funds for the "building of a new Negro hospital," which opened in 1951. As early as 1922, there was a small facility with forty beds for African Americans with TB, and the new facility had capacity for 204 beds. While this accomplishment made for better health to be accessible for all, it also kept the extreme segregation firmly in place. The majority of tuberculosis hospitals across the nation were segregated, but because of Mississippi's history, the segregation had a deeper, more sinister meaning. There is documentation, however, that as of 1968, once civil rights laws had been passed, this hospital was integrated. In the Prentiss newspaper interview, Dr. Boswell spoke about raising a million dollars to build the hospital for Black people and the difficulty of hiring Black physicians.

I had no knowledge of these additional TB hospitals, and as far as I know, we children at the preventorium did not know there was another tuberculosis hospital for Black people on the medical campus. I never saw any evidence of it in 1959–1960 when I was there. Were there Black children there? Were they allowed outside? How were they treated?

Dr. Henry Boswell was praised for founding the tuberculosis sanitorium and the preventorium. He was praised for implementing the "Fresh Air" method for "at risk" children who were patients at the preventorium. Boswell was a dedicated doctor and wanted better health for all Mississippians. His goal was clear, and he believed he was doing the correct thing for the health of the state's residents. Dr. Boswell, in fact, had contracted TB as a young man and received a "rest cure" in a facility in Texas in 1910, before he became the director of the Mississippi Tuberculosis Hospital in 1918.

Many children and parents were proud of the benefits they saw in the physical improvement of their children who had been at the preventorium. Was it a class issue or a regional one where southerners proudly proclaim their oddities like characters in novels?

Over the years, I sometimes shamefacedly attempted to tell someone about my time in the preventorium, but I couldn't bear the horrified looks or worse, the sense that I was not normal. I often heard judgmental and condescending reactions that "of course a place like Mississippi would have a preventorium." After all, Mississippi has a reputation for not just racism but extreme eccentricity. But preventoria were widespread nationally during the worst years of the TB epidemic.

I still take a deep breath before I tell someone about the pre-ventorium. Most people are very careful to keep their expressions neutral, but I still feel of shame at having spent so much time at a place that others now view as a eugenics experiment, or a kind of mental institution, or a place found only in that eccentric land, Mississippi.

Once, while at college, I heard myself mention the preventorium. It was just after a boy had asked me for a date. As I suddenly and unexpectedly blurted out that I had been a patient there, I could hear another voice in my head telling me to be silent, especially as I observed his face. How and why I let this information escape, I don't know. It was actually the first time since I was a child that I had even said the word "preventorium." He wanted to know more. As I described it, he slowly shook his head and kept saying in disbelief, "No place like that really existed, did it?" and "Why were you really there?"

And then, he didn't want to go on a date with me anymore.

I once read an article that said each time we access a memory, we alter it. But if we *don't* try to bring back those memories, where do they go? For me, they arose in the night, unbidden and unwelcome, just as I was about to fall asleep. They seemed to lie in wait and to leap into my mind with ever more startling clarity. Since I left, I have relived moments from the preventorium over and over. They flood into my mind just as I try to forget. When I see the photos in the social media posts by former patients as we share our pasts, they make me remember all the punishments and humiliations we observed. For some, sharing these stories and photos perhaps lessens the pain, but it does not lessen it for me. When these memories come to me at night, I must leave my bed and go to a window to look at the sky. Gazing at the sky, seeing the stars, moon, and clouds, helps to sweep away the horror of the film replaying in my brain.

For fifteen months, the preventorium was all I knew of the world. For the children there, the preventorium *was* the world. Perhaps that is why many of us remember the building as enormous. A common reaction upon visiting the old preventorium building is surprise at just how small it really is. As children, it filled the universe.

In 1959, it was a time of Jim Crow laws and emerging civil rights action in Mississippi. But we were sequestered in our white world of bloomers, hospital routines, and strict adults. Time stood still for us as we went about our daily routines, a schedule that had been determined thirty years earlier. No doubt the same routine continued until its closure with little variation. It was another dimension, a time warp where the same day repeated over and over.

I brought home with me an acute sense of emotional isolation. I often dreamt of floating, and I argued with people who told me this was a sign of trauma. I saw it as a mystical talent. As an incessant reader, I argued with my college professors about the characters in books who were categorized as "alienated" or "isolated." When we read Camus's *The Stranger*, everyone in class explained Meursault as psychologically alienated from other people and the world at large, lacking in normal emotions. They quoted essays and criticism that he did not react to events or to his environment in a "normal" way and that he felt disconnected from life. I vehemently argued that he was quiet, alone in himself, and observing, while trying to understand the situation at hand, his own emotions, and the actions of others. My professor, intrigued, gave me extra credit for my stubborn defense of him. But while I might identify with the isolation of people like Meursault, I did not understand or condone the casual violence in the book because I had already seen too much arbitrary cruelty.

And all of us as children at the preventorium missed out on many normal family interactions. We were stripped of normal childhood experiences, formed by a strict routine. When I returned to our family, I could neither readily become accustomed to the daily routine nor easily interact with neighborhood children and adults. I could not easily fit into larger family reunions until my teen years. I often hid from others, family as well as our neighbors, making sure to always have a book with me to read, and I avoided having to play games I had never learned. And while friends happily went off to summer camps, I was horrified at the idea of going away.

Only recently have I been able to understand the cruelty of separating children from families in the name of health. It took me many years to understand that I was not to blame for having been sent to the preventorium. I have also come to acknowledge my own difficulty in facing the darkness behind this experience. First, I hid the experience out of shame, and then I endlessly repeated how I had had a fine experience there, that I had not been emotionally affected by it, that it was like a fun summer camp, even though I had never attended a summer camp. I couldn't imagine a camp being fun, as my vision of camp was intertwined with the preventorium.

But at camp, they don't cut your hair like everyone else's, make you walk in tightly controlled lines with hands on hips, force you to wear the same exact clothes, and keep you tightly under control except for short periods at playtime. Adults, especially in the tuberculosis era, didn't view it that way at all but saw the routine as a matter of life and death.

And it was painful to think that my mother, overwhelmed at the sudden death and absence of my father, could not take care of me. Growing up, there were times when I wondered if my being at the preventorium meant that I had had discharged some unknown moral obligation.

As I grew older, I heard myself, over and over, telling people about the preventorium. I would hesitantly begin, show them a photo, and wait for a reaction. It feels like a judgment of *me* even though I was a child with no choice. I expect and often see and expression that broadcasts, "Something was really wrong with her." They ask me, was it like prison? Did this really take place in the United States? Was it eugenics? Or they tell me a story about a worse hospital experience or send me articles about institutions where even more terrible things happened.

The preventorium shaped me. It seeped into my bones, my spirit, and my thoughts.

Children's emotional and psychological needs were not considered during the height of the fearful tuberculosis era—the focus was on physical health to prevent any of us from contracting TB. But institutionalization took a toll on all the children. One former patient I spoke with in August 2018 observed that those children whose lives were truly in danger valued the preventorium as saving their lives; others who were there only because their parents were patients in the tuberculosis hospital did not have a favorable view. I understand this interpretation but cannot reconcile the emotional impact in either case.

At the preventorium, I learned early on to observe objectively. Children study the adults around them, learn from them, and adapt to established norms. Or, they do not conform and suffer the consequences. The focus in 1959, when I was there, was on conformity and routine. If we stepped outside these boundaries, the paddle or public humiliation awaited. To this day, I am a master at appearing to connect, emotionally, socially, and deeply with others while I am standing away from myself watching everything. I always assumed everyone did this.

When I am experiencing the most extreme disassociation, I often find that after even very pleasant social events, I am unable to recall conversations I have had with friends even when that friend recounted to me how meaningful the talk had been. I sometimes feel emotionally cut off from everyone, even as we are all enjoying a social event together. To explain this disassociation, especially to myself, is almost impossible, except that I did this very thing every hour of every day for nearly a year and a half as a child. I thus formed a protective habit of doing so. When waking at night, often with a memory of the fearful nights at the preventorium, I worry I have become selfish from my experience with this continued disassociation.

At a very early age, I learned there is no real safety in life. Children can be taken from their homes and mothers. Anything can happen to anyone in a heartbeat. At the preventorium, I learned to be wary of what the world offered.

My brother's description of culture and social behavior at that time resonates strongly with my experience of children's emotional needs not being recognized. We lived in a culture then, that if a family had a problem, it was not discussed. In those years, the state itself, with the exception of a small population in the capital of Jackson, was extremely rural and often poor. Jackson, even as the capital, did not become a bustling city until many decades later. The ethos of rural life carried over in how children were treated, perceived, and expected to behave.

He made me laugh by describing southern rules that illustrate where children ranked socially when he and I were small. There was an unspoken rule for when fried chicken, a favorite of almost everyone, was served for dinner. In the majority of households, children were served the "lesser" pieces of chicken: the wings, necks, backs, and if lucky, the drumsticks. Only adults were allowed to choose the larger, more succulent pieces. This was the pecking order of households, where children were expected to be silent and behave.

The disconnect between the cheerful, health-focused version of the preventorium presented in reports and articles, and the specific, individual isolation that all of us experienced was profound and little understood. I have read the informational brochures and reports that extoll the efficacy of the "Fresh Air Method," and tout the cheery togetherness of the children, their enjoyment of the holiday seasons, the school, the playground, and the opportunity to be among so many other children. We were lined up for group photos, and we all smiled. We understood the unspoken expectations to appear happy. Perhaps some of the children *were* happy. So many were not. I understood all too well that I had no choice. I coped and adjusted as best I could. But I also became extremely disassociated, emotionally passive, and indifferent as I watched as other children sometimes fought against the rigid structure. I believed that I was being observant and objective, but I was actually disassociated, uncoupled from my emotions. This enabled me to survive. I learned not to miss my mother and forgot about my brother and anyone else associated with my home in Jackson. I learned not to analyze the reasons for the behavior of the staff, the children, or anyone else. I interacted with the other children when we were on the playground and formed one close friendship. There was little to no real interaction with any of the little boys there. They were a distant group in the ward on the other side of the main hall.

And because I was there longer than most children, I had great trouble reentering all aspects of my life at home.

When I look at the staged, happy photos in newspapers, and the more informal, spontaneous photos that families took, I see children performing for adults' attention. The informal photos were taken during some of the rare, truly free time for us to be ourselves. The children, aware that they, as well as the adults were being observed, took liberties they might not take if it were just preventorium staff and patients. Little boys made faces behind adults' backs, little girls whispered and giggled secrets that normally they would never have had the opportunity to share.

In the dark of the night, I often think about my mother's visits and how I tried to please her by pretending to be happy. Perhaps the preventorium did save my physical self. I was told it did. But those first weeks, in the dark night in a foreign place, I was the most alone I had ever been or ever will be again. I felt utterly abandoned.

When I show someone a photo of me at age six in my white bloomers, blunt pixie cut, and bare feet, with other children around me, the shock on the faces of those viewing the photos sometimes

Susan with fan

angers me as I view myself through their eyes. I have come to realize that it is shame and not anger I feel.

The preventorium is now gone, but other practices have taken their place. Children are taken from parents at borders; children are taken from their homes. In the case of the preventorium, all was done in the name of health with the best intentions. But we were robbed of our individuality. What is the first thing that is done to a prisoner? Haircuts, uniforms, routinized days and nights, and punishment for stepping outside the established rules.

As soon as I feel the anger and shame, I also feel guilt. I was alive, cared for physically, and as I matured, I knew what it cost my mother to send me there.

There is no way to reconcile this.

Epilogue
A Last Wish

What I want is to live in a world where children will never again
be turned over by their parents or at the recommendations of their
physicians to an institution with no accountability to the parents. To
the children of the preventorium, I feel a special kinship, whether
or not they can relate to my experiences there. If they remember it
quite differently, so be it. They survived it in their own way, and they
get a full pass from me.
—**MIKE SANDERS,** patient at the Mississippi Preventorium, 1963

Acknowledgments

Many thanks go to dear friends who supported my writing this memoir, especially Anne Mazer, who encouraged, inspired, and supported me from the beginning, reading so many drafts and offering valuable suggestions. Thank you also to Carol Kammen, Caroline Cox, Helena Viramontes, Leslie Daniels, and Zee Zahava, all of whom inspired and advised me. Thank you to my tight-knit group of lifelong friends, who read early sections and listened to my stories of my experience, especially Gwen, Andrea, Joellen, Elizabeth, Betsy, Debbie, and Sarah. Thank you to Debra Wilson for her advice in using older photos. Thank you to Carol Clemente at the Bartle Library at SUNY Binghamton for her assistance in obtaining research materials and to Tom Burns at the Tompkins County Public Library in Ithaca, New York, for his assistance in obtaining documents. Many thanks go to Dr. Cynthia Connolly for her research, book, and publications about preventoria and her willingness to read my manuscript and to write a foreword. Thank you to the reference librarians at the Mississippi Department of Archives and History and the Mississippi Library Commission. A special thanks goes to Cornell professors Lamar Herrin, whose encouragement and creative writing class provided the first opportunity to give words to my experience, and Kenneth McClane, who read early drafts and whose encouragement was so important. Thank you to Lisa McMurtray at the University Press of Mississippi for answering so many questions about the publishing process. Thanks to the Minnesota Northwoods Writers Conference and instructor Meera Subramanian for her guidance. Thank you to author Laura Davis for her memoir workshop. Thank you to former patient Mike Sanders, who gave me permission to quote from his writings of his time at the preventorium. Thank you to former fellow preventorium patients Judy Andrews Callender, Judy Burchfield Rowe, B. J. Barnes, Cindy Hale, and Judy Sadler-Bunch, who shared their memories and experiences with me. Thank you to Elsa Clift Everling for permission to include her preventorium photos of the dining room and classroom. Thank you to every member of the Magee, Mississippi, Preventorium Facebook page for the support and inspiration. While we all had varying experiences there, we have a shared history.

I cannot thank my brother, Ned, enough for his encouragement and support, for his stories about how he spent time at the preventorium while our mother was visiting me, and for information about my return home after the preventorium.

Thank you also to my mother, who saved my life.

Finally, thank you to Chris. Without your love, enthusiastic encouragement, and support, none of this would have been possible.

Bibliography

Boswell, Iola. Interview with John Jones and Martha Monaghan, March 8, 1979. Jackson: Mississippi Department of Archives and History, February 1983.

Boswell Regional Center (website), State of Mississippi, 2022, https://www.brc.ms.gov/.

Calder, Marvin R. *Mississippi State Sanatorium: History 1916–1976.* Florence, MS: Messenger Press, 1986.

Connolly, Cynthia A. *Saving Sickly Children: The Tuberculosis Preventorium in American Life, 1909–1970.* New Brunswick, NJ: Rutgers University Press, 2008.

Eschenbrenner, Donna. "Preventorium Built to Prevent TB in Tompkins County." *Ithaca Journal,* August 3, 2013, 9A.

Genova, Lisa. *Remember: The Science of Memory and the Art of Forgetting.* New York: Harmony Books, 2021.

Gray, Archie L. *Forty-Second Biennial Report, Being the Eighty-Third and Eighty-Fourth Annual Reports of the State Board of Health of the State of Mississippi,* July 1, 1959–June 30, 1961. Jackson: Mississippi State Department of Health, 1959–1961.

Groves, J. B., and M. C. Trotter. "The Mississippi State Tuberculosis Sanatorium and the Evolution of Thoracic Surgery in Mississippi." *Journal of Mississippi State Medical Association* 55, no.6 (June 2014): 180–86. PMID: 25137770.

Kleinschmidt, H. E. "What Is a Preventorium?" *American Journal of Public Health* 20, no.7 (1930): 715–21.

Mississippi State Sanitorium: A Book of Information about Tuberculosis and Its Treatment in Mississippi. Sanatorium, MS: Mississippi State Sanatorium and the Mississippi Tuberculosis Association, 1939.

Mullen, Phil. "Preventorium Pupil's Dad Lauds Institution." *Jackson Clarion-Ledger,* January 24, 1960, 10.

Pettus, Gary. "Once Sickly Children Recall Preventorium." *Jackson Clarion-Ledger,* June 19, 2010, 1, 4.

"A Pound of Cure." *Newsweek,* March 2, 1953, 78.

Skelton, Billy. "Most Enthusiastic Alumni in State for 'Preventorium,'" *Jackson Clarion-Ledger,* February 4, 1968, 45.

"Tops in the Nation." *Carraway's Store and Theatre News,* no. 16 (August 18, 1951).

Van der Kolk, Bessel. *The Body Keeps the Score: Brain, Mind, and Body in the Healing of Trauma.* New York: Penguin, 2014.

Social Media Resources

Magee Mississippi Preventorium, member 2009–present. Members are former patients who post information about experiences. https://www.facebook.com/groups/69103809566/.

"TB/Asthma Sanatorium—Sanatorium MS, 1962." Mississippi Preventorium. Video misdated 1962; date is 1959 or 1960. YouTube video, 4:00. https://www.youtube.com/watch?v=q9OouG_pr8w.

About the Author

Photo by Christine McNamara

When she was six years old, Susan Annah Currie spent fifteen months as a patient in the preventorium hospital in Magee, Mississippi, where children were allowed visits from parents only twice a month, and adhered to a strict daily routine, called the "Fresh Air Method."

Susan is a native Mississippian, born in Jackson in 1953. She obtained a BA in English from Belhaven College and attended graduate school for English Literature at the University of Mississippi. In 1979, she moved to Ithaca, New York, and obtained a masters in library science from the University of Buffalo. She was an academic librarian for close to thirty years, including Cornell University and SUNY Binghamton University Libraries. In 2009, she was chosen to be the director of the historic Tompkins County Public Library in Ithaca.

Ironically, she now lives fewer than ten miles away from what was once a preventorium. The Cayuga Nature Center, just outside Ithaca, New York, opened in 1939 as the Cayuga Preventorium with assistance from the WPA. It existed for twenty-one years.

This memoir has been living and breathing inside of her since 1960.